AF879766

# Lazy is Good:

# Do it Once, Do it Right, Don't do it Again!

## A quick start guide to delivering better projects

**William R. Wimberly** – Bridging the Quality Gap

Copyright © 2016 v3 William R. Wimberly & wwPublishing

ALL RIGHTS RESERVED. No part of this work covered by the copyright herein may be reproduced, transmitted, stored, or used in any form or by any means graphic, electronic, or mechanical, including but not limited to photocopying, recording, scanning, digitizing, or taping, Web distribution, information networks, or information storage and retrieval systems, except as permitted under Section 107 or 108 of the 1976 United States Copyright Act, without written permission of the author.

Reviewers may quote brief passages to be printed in magazine or newspaper.

The right for limited academic classroom use is allowed as long as proper credit to this work is maintained.

ISBN-10: 0-9979372-0-3
ISBN-13: 978-0-9979372-0-6

This book is designed to provide information and guidance in regard to the subject matter covered. It is sold with the understanding that the author is not engaged in rendering counseling, legal, or other professional services.

CreateSpace Independent Publishing Platform
Edited and Published by
wwPublishing

www.williamwimberly.com/books

www.williamwimberly.com/brand

http://www.linkedin.com/in/wrwimberly

Yoda in Star Wars said it best when it comes to producing Quality:

We know how to do it – we can do it – but as Luke Skywalker says to Yoda "I don't believe it."

We don't act on what we know but on what we believe, so Yoda's reply says it all –

**"That is why you fail!"**

# ♣ Dedication ♣

To all who believe that Quality is a way of life and not a job,
this book is dedicated to you.

To all who work daily to make Quality a way of life,
this book is dedicated to you.

And

To all who want to learn how to make Quality a way of life,
this book is dedicated to you.

This publication is designed to provide the author's opinions and specific point-of-view from his real world experiences. While the experiences come from specific work environments, every effort has been made to generalize the information to not reference any specific organization. The information is accurate only to my experiences. The author has used due care and diligence in providing proper citation and credit for the works of others, but many of the quotes and saying are a collection over the years and the actual sources are not known; there is no intent to misuse any copyrighted materials and doing so is unintentional and the author thanks others for allowing the use of any such materials for the education and learning of others.

# ♣ Acknowledgements ♣

I want to give a special thanks to my students who "got it" and whose words keep me going, for example:

> Dear professor Wimberly,
>
> You have given us a great opportunity to learn a lot of life lessons from your experience and provided us challenging assignments... You have brought positive change in each one of us.
>
> Some of us have realized already, but some students will understand only when they realize the value of those life lessons...
>
> We all might be taking different professions. Thanks to your efforts, we would be doing it better. You will be remembered throughout our lives.
>
> Thank you for helping us to become better than ourselves. It's a great noble act mainly because you have done that even though you know many students don't appreciate it.

# ♣ Forward ♣

I was stuck on more traditional titles and hated each idea… then Kristina suggested this one – her philosophy on life and a great title for this book.

• • •

This great title came from Kristina Hernandez, a former co-worker; this is her philosophy on life and a great title for a book.

• • •

I am saddened by how many companies insist that they do not have time to do it right and will do it over again later. At what price? The landscape is littered with the remains of failed companies that **never made it to the point they had time to do it over!**

• • •

**Only when QUALITY is the goal of each component do you have a situation where "the whole is greater than the sum of the parts."**

• • •

As you read through this book, you may be wondering how some of the topics deal with QUALITY? The answer is simple. Properly performed, Quality Assurance is a part of all aspects of everything we do. The strength of the strongest chain is determined by its weakest link. **Only** when QUALITY is the goal of each task or component do you have a situation where "the whole is greater than the sum of the parts."

There are hundreds of books on all these topics. This book is not to give that information again ... but to add my first-person real-world additions. Each chapter is a short narrative about some of my experiences and the things I have learned that may be new to you or a new way of looking at or thinking about a topic – BUT ALWAYS WORK TO ADD QUALITY.

# ♣About the Author♣

First, I am not a writer, as you will see for yourself as you read this book. I was once told by the Founder and CEO of a technical writing company to never call myself a writer – but as a technical person, I was a better writer than most technical personnel. I did not invent the ideas and concepts I discuss, as I say in my brand I am **innovative** versus creative, but I did spend my career making them WORK for organizations and improving the outcomes and this book is about some of the ways I did that. The only new concept – to IT folks at least – may be the one about using my experience and knowledge in human biological rhythms to verify other study results on productivity (chapter 3 - Productivity).

Second, any mistakes you might find in this book were put there intentionally for your amusement and practice in Quality Assurance. ☺

Third, if you believe number 2 I have a bridge to sell you!

With that out of the way....

**Whatever you do today ... Make it worth this ...**

A question I often ask is ….
If you paid me a million dollars an hour to work for you, what is the only thing my million dollars cannot buy me?

**The hour of my life I just gave up!**

To me, that says that whatever I have just done must be something I would want to receive as a customer - QUALITY.

• • •

**The motivation for QUALITY must come from within you – it is not something you can "add on."**

• • •

A story I tell my students about work-life balance is to:

Get a tall clear plastic tube, go to the web and do some research on your expected remaining lifetime (from your birth year and age now), and take that number of years and multiple by fifty-two for the number of weekend days (Saturday and Sunday) you have remaining; put that number of marbles in the tube and mark with a felt marker the level of the marbles.
Each Saturday and Sunday, remove one marble from the tube.

• • •

**The greatest gift you have been handed in life is <u>TIME</u> – use it wisely! Make EVERYTHING you do the most important thing you can do with your time at that moment.**

• • •

At first it may not seem like a big deal, but very soon, you will understand what those hours mean that you give up and what they are worth!

## My Personal Brand

The modern concept for "job hunting" is to NOT hunt for a job but to have others come to you (be recruited). We also use to talk about the 30-second elevator pitch of what you do or are looking for career (job) wise.

The biggest and most successful companies already know both are combined in your brand. Develop your personal brand and you can talk it, show it, post it, and others know quickly who you are and what you can do for them.

In my staffing class I spend time on 1st Impressions (others ideas of you and <u>their</u> values) and Reputation (your idea of you and <u>your</u> values).

You want how you see yourself to match how others see you … I spend several nights and a homework assignment on developing a brand (see example concept for my personal brand below).

What do I want to be known for, how do I want to be seen by others – my **Reputation**.

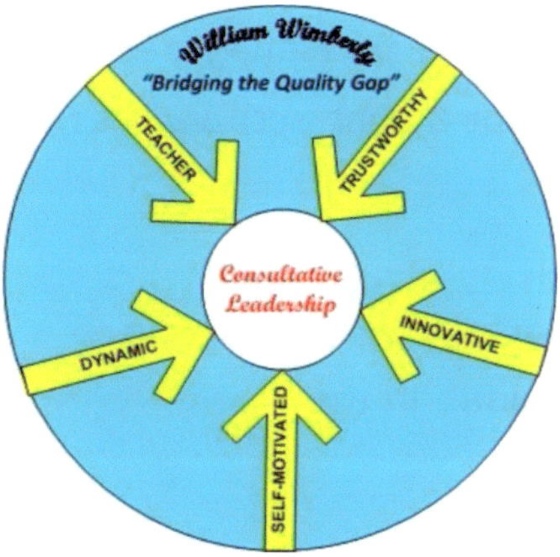


www.williamwimberly.com/brand

## THE ONLY CONTRACT I TRUST

The only contract no lawyer in the world can break is a handshake. Only the two people who make it can break it. That makes this the most powerful contract there is – it is bound by your **honor and reputation** – the second most important thing you have to give (after your time)!

## QA is who I am, not what I do...

I am asked often when I decided to go into QA as a profession. My answer is I didn't decide to go into QA, it is who I am. I don't put on my QA hat at 8:00AM and take it off at 5:00PM.

I was once said to be "the most naturally QA person they had every seen" by a QA Manager and QA Lead who interviewed me for a contract; and yes, I was hired for the contract.

But this "natural" QA personality did not start as an adult in the workplace.

**I didn't go into QA,**

**I was born QA.**

In elementry school, maybe 3rd grade, I did an art assignment – not as assigned by the teacher – but so well I was noted for it and received an A.

In 7th grade shop class, I was called out by the teacher for having followed the directions precisely in making a simple screwdriver.

And in college, I was the only student who ever did a specific assignment correctly; the instructor did not even have a lecture for it – the lecture was only to teach how to do it correctly after having done it wrong the first time.

And a project (program) I wrote was the only one the Professor could not break.

To my knowledge, no code I wrote ever failed in production. Why? Because once I took off my "developer" hat I put on my "QA" hat and tore it apart if I could.

This is by no means a comperhensive list of examples, but shows how the attitude of QA has been with me for as long as I can remember, even as a child.

I started my career in IT as a developer. From there to many other roles, in organizations from small to very large, and in many industries. I say that the only two roles I have not performed, by my choice, are as a DBA or a network engineer.

Throughout all my roles and titles, QA was there, driving the way I worked, shaping my vision of the work, and giving me a purpose – to make the best product or service I could for the customer – what I expect AS A CUSTOMER...

# ♣ Table of Contents ♣

# ♣ Introduction ♣

**We are really bad at what we do! We know how to do it better, but realities today make it hard. It has to be faster, not better!**

**We have been conditioned to expect and accept less than the best – so that is what we get!**

The order of the sections and chapters may seem different – yes, they are different from other texts. I have placed them not in the order typically considered as the sequence of events for a project, but in the order that I think they should be thought of to produce the best QUALITY.

Since "**the only constant in life is change,"** variations in implementation may be applied for different projects, but the concepts should always be applied in this general sequence. This constant change leads me to the next thing I know to be true "**Those who fail to PLAN, plan to FAIL**." You will see throughout this book the idea of planning – planning for QUALITY!

I want to start with something I seen only in a few textbooks but that I learned very early on in my career and it has proven to be one of the best lessons I ever learned; I use it every day for everything I do – **CRUD** – Create, Read, Update, and Delete.

To me it is a lesson to take a full 360 degree look at everything. I first learned it in figuring out a "bug" in a program that had to do with missing requirements. But now I ask "**did you CRUD that?**" for everything I do!

I have found this one simple question can prevent so many issues from every happening as I go through each step of a project.
Note: What you should be asking may not always be Create, Read, Update, or Delete? For each activity you may substitute the appropriate terms. It is the concept of looking at each thing you are doing from that 360 degree point of view and asking yourself if you thought of all that you can to make it correct. Did I consider all the options or all of the consequences?

Always think globally (strategically) at least two levels above where you are now and act locally (operationally) – your specific role.

# ♣THE Problem♣

Yes, we in IT are bad at what we do! Wow, how can I make such a general, blanket statement like that? Because the numbers support it.

• • •

**We must be better!**

• • •

And no, this is **not** true of every single organization, project, or worker. Then we would be perfectly bad at it, and we are not that. I have shown at company after company that I worked for, both big and small, that you can take the concepts, methodologies, procedures, processes, and guidelines and adapt & adopt them to beat the norm … and do it better or cheaper!
The evidence is there, the proof is there, clear to those that are willing to look and listen. So, why are we so bad at it?

I don't have the answer or answers! I just see examples every day of so many different reasons, from not caring, not understanding, not being willing to admit you do not know everything, not listening, … example after example.

There are the shining examples of how to do it right! I hope my book will make you want to find those examples and learn to do it better and better every day – continuous process improvement (CPI)!

## What I See

There are an untold number of studies and reports on the state of IT success and failure. Depending on the report and the year, the numbers change, but all the ones I trust show we have a lot of room for improvement.

Some even show us improving over the years. My personal observation on this is that the best are improving so much more than the rest that they bring the overall numbers up. This is just my guess; I have not done professional research on this to establish a methodology to support my observations. But, in my every day, overall view, I see mainly no real improvement.

• • •

Some people use statistics like drunks use lampposts, for support, not illumination.

*Source Unknown*

• • •

That is why I am citing the specific work and numbers I am. They feel right to what I see every day. I acknowledge that others will see it differently and have different numbers.

**As QA, I await and will welcome the day that I am totally wrong on this!**

# By The Numbers

In my class on *Management Information Systems*, I use the Gartner Report as my example. Following are the numbers and I will comment afterwards.

**2009**

- 90% of all IT project were delivered late
- 50% of all IT project were delivered over budget
- 60% of all IT project failed to meet objectives

Reference:

http://www.sqsi.com/downloads/healthcheck_en.pdf

**2010**

- **90%** of all IT project were delivered late (**Time**)
- **50%** of all IT project were delivered over budget (**Costs**)
- **50%** of all IT project failed to meet objectives, not meet expectations. **(Quality)**
- **Software bugs cost the US economy an estimated $59.5 Billion annually (0.6% of US GDP, 2002).** A survey commissioned by NIST.

http://www.scribd.com/doc/53494909/It-Key-Metrics-Data-2011-Key-208272 ---- Publication Date: 17 December 2010

**2011**

- 43% of all IT project are delivered late.

Info-Tech Research Group says its 95% (see reference below)

- 33% of all IT project are delivered over budget
- 6% of all IT project fail to meet objectives; projects are cancelled before delivery – key metric

http://caseysoftware.com/blog/95-of-it-projects-not-delivered-on-time

Note: I looked at later numbers as well, but feel this set defines the point I want to make and the later numbers show the same uneven trends.

For so many of the small companies I have worked for the numbers were 100%, 100%, 100%. But as I said above, I think a few really good organizations raise the reported numbers overall.

For ease of teaching, I use the **2010** numbers – **90/50/50**. Note the decline between 2009 and 2010 in meeting objectives (quality).

These numbers show we have only a **2.5% success** rate … a 97.5% failure rate for projects! **We ARE bad at what we do – by the numbers!**

Given the previous numbers and my own observations and those of everyone I speak with, I question the 2011 numbers. Even the report questions and shows a large decrease in the first metric (delivered late). I also see no way we dropped from 50/50% to 33/6% in one year.

• • •

**Software bugs cost the US economy an estimated $59.5 Billion annually (0.6% of US GDP, 2002).**

***NIST Study***

• • •

• • •

**Believe you can do better as the largest room in the world is the room for improvement.**

***Lionnel N. Yamentou***

• • •

Just these three years of numbers shows how much variance can be found in the numbers and how hard it is to evaluate how we are really doing. But all show we have lots of room for improvement. While I more often see numbers higher than the 2010 numbers, for purposes of discussion I will use them as the "standard."

## A Story

I use this story to explain to my classes the issue involved here.

I am the project manager and I go to the stakeholders/customers or financial folks and tell them on this "million" dollar project I was just assigned to, there is a 90% chance the delivery will be late AND a 50% chance I will be over budget and need MORE money AND there is a 50% chance after all that the project will NOT meet your objects for it.

**AND countless times per year, we are told to go ahead anyway! WHY?**

• • •

**Could these numbers help explain why the US ranks 125th in GDP growth per capita –**

***see CoQ chapter***

• • •

Assuming all three variables are at play on each project, each project only stands a **2.5**% chance of meeting ALL three and a successful project requires meeting all three.

What motive is there to improve? I can tell you many stories of failures where the person in charge actually got a raise or promoted! WOW!

I will not pretend to have the answers to WHY. But I do see the results everyday and I have proven repeatly that the results can be better. I have done it!

**WHY do we accept these numbers? That to me is the real question?**

A quick Google search, May 19, 2013, came up with these numbers – something to think about:

- The US ranks 1st in wine consumption
- The US ranks 10th in economic freedom
- The US ranked 31 of 74 in mathematics, 23 of 74 in science, 17 of 74 in reading
- **The U.S. was ranked 17th in an [overall] assessment of the education systems of 50 countries**

**Are we beginning to see THE PROBLEM here?**

# Part One

## ♣The Fundamentals♣

# Chapter One

## ♣Human Resource Management♣

• • •

**The biggest mistake companies make in hiring is they hire for SKILLS but fire for PERSONALITY.**

***Peggy Roberts, VP/Senior Recruiter***

• • •

# Introduction

We have taken a look at the "The Problem" and have a basic idea about what it is, so where do we start to fix it? We start with hiring the right people!

Easier said than done ... **we can also be very bad at that!**

There must be thousands/millions or more pages on the HRM topic. I will focus on listing some of what I see as the biggest issues of quality and briefly detail a few. In addition, I will add my specific contribution to the topic of salary and compensation – my comparison spreadsheet.

## Hire for Skills ....

I start with this quote from a friend and HRM professional with years of experience. This is maybe one of the biggest issues today; I see it every day in my own experience. A full discussion could take a whole book itself. So, for now I just want to point it out and make a few comments.

• • •

**The biggest mistake an organization makes is to hire for skills and fire for personality.**

*Peggy Roberts, HRM professional and friend*

I understand companies get tens to hundreds of resumes for each position, but hiring smarter is an issue of quality...

resume review by key word software, review by HR personnel looking for key words and not understanding what is actually needed for the position cause problems. However, the worst is the hiring of personnel and not understanding this "biggest mistake" is the "root of the evil" so to speak.

Who were the first programmers, muscians and mathematicians, because they could think in a certain way and learn new concepts.
If someone can learn and fits into your organization personality wise, don't throw them out because of experience, or not, on a specific tool(s) – **can they think and learn is what is important!**

• • •

**The key and most important lesson is to "learn how to learn." As technology changes (the only constant) you must know how to learn anew to keep up.**

***Author unknown***

• • •

It is said that the generals always fight the last war, i.e., the one they learned how to fight with the tools they knew. The same might be said for hiring for the future. While the concepts, techniques, theriories, basic principles, etc., that I discuss here may stay the same or evolve somewhat, the **technologies** will change (the only constant).

Many of the technologies we teach in school will be outdated by the time the students even guadate and for sure within a few short years after they start working.

We are teaching and then hiring for the **now** jobs ....

Found on Internet, source unknown

Since personnel turnover is arguability the single largest expense to an organization, for long term success, **we must hire for the ability to retrain and the desire to LEARN HOW TO LEARN**!

## It's the Whole Compensation Package
**Not just the salary!**

The first thing everyone focuses on is the salary or the rate for a contract. Unfortunately, that is often times the only thing they focus on.
In the case of contracts without benefits, almost the standard anymore, you must also consider what you are missing in benefits to determine the required rate.

• • •

It's much more than the salary.

What is important to you? What do you need to make overall to accept a job and not leave the first time a higher salary comes along?

Remember the first one to bring up salary loses – especially if it is you, the applicant. An exception is when the position is from a recruiter and you want to know if the salary/rate is even worth your time to apply. Ask away, but this still means you must know what your minimum is.

How do I know mine? I created a spreadsheet to evaluate different positions on an objective basis. It also allows for some major subjective values to be compared side-by-side for ease of comparison.

And once I have determined that a position meets my financial requirements, I still sleep on it for at least one night to allow my "gut feel" to have time to weight in, usually 3:00AM in the morning for me.

## My Comparison SpreadSheet

So how do I quickly determine if the financial aspect of an opportunity works? My spreadsheet compares my criteria, currently about 100 lines long. It provides both a net to gross evaluation for the specific position and a comparison of that position to a baseline one, including a bottom line dollar difference on selected items.

The spreadsheet allows me to compare both direct hire positions with benefits and contract positions with partial or no benefits. As part of the direct versus contract positions it uses my specific effective tax rate for both types of employment; the effective tax rate takes into account many other factors all on a single line of the spreadsheet.

• • •

**Depending on what is important to you, the total compensation package can offset straight salary by thousands of dollars.**

• • •

The example shown below has been edited to preserve some individual criteria, some lines are redacted, and salaries chosen to reflect how the bottom line is affected by the factors shown. The actual formulas used in the calculations would be adjusted to your specific requirements.

Some key items to note are:

- Subjective items like "Rec center or Gym" could be made objective by adding a dollar value to a gym membership that could be saved.
- The A2 value for calculating mileage costs can be adjusted for your actual costs (if known) versus a general value.
- The estimated commute time is used in calculations that are redacted for this example. But the mileage each way and adjusted days off are important as well as the vacation & holiday numbers, I adjust for the days I am not driving to work (QA is about the details).

The bottom line is that the same, or even a lower or higher salary, may or may not be the best overall package depending on what is important to you. Having this actual information provides another avenue of negotiation for a position or for a "raise" request; "hey boss, I don't really need a salary increase but how about a work at home day (saves commute costs) or more days off (saves both commute costs and adds to quality of life)."

You might also include items like cell phone costs; I choose to have my own for privacy reasons, or if you get a company vehicle you would adjust for only what you pay out of pocket.

The sample below gives a general idea that it is much more than just the salary. Be sure to look at the "Real Net Dollars on Selected Costs" versus the "Base Salary" lines.

| Company Name: | Baseline Company - | Test Company | Test Company |
|---|---|---|---|
| | Direct Hire | Direct Hire | Direct Hire |
| Note: cost per mile to drive = (see below) | | | |
| $0.80 | | | Family on Dental Ins. |
| Base Salary - yearly: | $91,000 | $84,864 | $91,000 |
| Base Salary - hourly (40 hour/wk): | $43.75 | $40.80 | $43.75 |
| Base Salary - hourly (Actual/Est. hours/wk): | $35.00 | $40.80 | $31.82 |
| TBD (free food etc.) - (added to salary) | $0.00 | $144.00 | $144.00 |
| Pay period: | LDM | 15th & LDM | 10th & 25th |
| Actual Expected Working Hrs: | 50 | 40 | 55 |
| Working Hours comments (1099 if applicable) | | | |
| **1099 type stuff** | $2,730.00 | $2,545.92 | $2,730.00 |
| **Total Employee Taxes** | **31,850.00** | **29,702.40** | **31,850.00** |
| Employee Federal Marginal Tax Rate (Your%) | $22,750.00 | $21,216.00 | $22,750.00 |
| Employee CA Marginal Tax Rate (Your%) | $9,100.00 | $8,486.40 | $9,100.00 |
| **Total 1099 Taxes** | **$29,120.00** | **$27,156.48** | **$29,120.00** |
| 1099 Federal Marginal Tax Rate (Your%) | $22,750.00 | $21,216.00 | $22,750.00 |
| 1099 CA Marginal Tax Rate (Your%) | $6,370.00 | $5,940.48 | $6,370.00 |
| Business Tax **(zero 0 for W2/Employee)** | $0.00 | $0.00 | $0.00 |
| Private life insurance costs /Year (minus) | $0.00 | $0.00 | $0.00 |
| Est. commute time - hrs/year | 686 | 239 | 311.25 |
| Est. commute time - hrs/day | 3.5 | 1 | 1.25 |
| Adjustments, e.g., 9/80 days off | **40** | 0 | 0 |
| Mileage (one way): | 40 | 12.5 | 11.5 |
| Driving cost @ current rate (see A2) | $12,544.00 | $4,780.00 | $5,781.60 |
| **Personal Car Usage Expected (miles/YR) (includes tp/from out of area job)** | 0 | 0 | 1500 |
| Rideshare / Train etc./ Tolls (below) - Annual: | $0 | $0 | $0 |
| Monthly Cost - fixed: | $0.00 | $0.00 | $0.00 |
| Co. Pymt (Monthly): | $0 | $0 | $0 |
| Parking &/or Toll Costs - Annual: | $0.00 | $0.00 | $0.00 |
| Parking &/or Toll fees/day | $0 | $0 | $0 |

| | | | |
|---|---|---|---|
| Benefits: | | | |
| Medical COSTS: | $495.00 | $135.00 | $475.00 |
| Monthly Cost: | $40.00 | $10.00 | $50.00 |
| Deductible (assumes 1 visit per year): | $15.00 | $15.00 | $15.00 |
| Max. Liability: | $1,500.00 | $1,500.00 | $4,500.00 |
| Family on coverage (deduct from Costs as possible savings) | $0.00 | $0.00 | $140.00 |
| Dental (cost/year): | $200.00 | $200.00 | $200.00 |
| Vision (cost/year): | $200.00 | $200.00 | $200.00 |
| Saving plan matching (**normed to 1 yrs value**): | 568.75 | 353.60 | 409.50 |
| Years to Full vesting | 4 | 6 | 5 |
| % matched (see Cal page): | 50% | 50% | 50% |
| Maximum % matched: | 5% | 5% | 4.5% |
| Free stocks provided: | No | No | No |
| est. @ $value * Stocks/yr | $0.00 | $0.00 | $0.00 |
| **POSSIBLE** Co. pd Profit sharing $ per year: | $4,550.00 | $2,000.00 | 0 |
| Co. paid retirement plan (Y/N) | No | No | No |
| Est. value for year XXXX | $0.00 | $0.00 | $0.00 |
| Credit Union: | no | yes | No |
| Vacation (days per year): | 15 | 11 | 5 |
| Holidays (days per year): | 9 | 10 | 6 |
| Vacation pay difference: | $0.00 | ($1,305.60) | ($3,500.00) |
| Holiday pay difference: | $0.00 | $326.40 | ($1,050.00) |
| PTO (accured only) used in calculations (Days) | 0.00 | 0.00 | 0.00 |
| Sick leave (NOT used in calculations): | 0 | 6 | 5 |
| Paid Jury/Witness days (if required) (NOT used in calculations): | 0 | 5 | 0 |
| Co. Pd Life Insurance: | 136,500 | 50,000 | 50,000 |
| LTD cost/month: | $0.00 | $31.90 | $0.00 |
| STD cost/month: | $0.00 | $0.00 | $0.00 |
| Education reimbursement $$/yr: | $0 | $0 | $0 |
| Additional costs to **substract** from salary: | $0 | $0 | $0 |
| Out of area housing expenses: | $0 | $0 | $0 |
| Out of area living expenses: | $0 | $0 | $0 |
| Out of area to/from travel costs: | $0 | $0 | $0 |
| Others not Shown | $0 | $0 | $0 |
| Dress Code: | Bus. Casual | Casual | Bus. Casual |
| Add your $value for cost/comfort of dress, e.g., Business Causal, Causal, etc.: | $500.00 | $0.00 | $500.00 |
| Smoking allowed: | No | No | No |
| Rec center or Gym: | No | yes | No |
| Used to calculate adjusted salary | | | |
| Adjusted Salary: | $215,949.75 | $146,376.28 | $143,512.21 |
| % of Base Salary: | 237% | 172% | 158% |
| Others not Shown | | | |
| % of Last adjusted salary | 100.00% | 67.78% | 66.46% |
| Others not Shown | | | |
| $ difference of Last adjusted salary: | $0.00 | ($69,573.47) | ($72,437.54) |
| per month $ difference | $0.00 | -$5,797.79 | -$6,036.46 |
| Others not Shown | | | |
| **Real NET dollars based on selected costs:** | **$73,762.25** | **$76,617.58** | **$80,703.90** |
| Real dollar difference based on selected items: {List your specific items here and add their line numbers to formula on line 93} | $0.00 Postive Number is Dollars | $2,855.33 | $6,941.65 |

See the difference in the "Real NET dollars…." That is your real money in the pocket.

## When you post a job ad

Try and reply to it as **real** applicants will … with unique or missing values … if you can't do it, how do expect them to?

**Do YOU test that an applicant can even apply to your job ad?**

I asked this question to a friend once after trying (the web site had serious faults and kept failing) to apply to a position where she works, one of the biggest in its industry in Southern California… in over 30 years in HR, she had never tried it. She is NOT alone.

If not every day, then every week, in applying to positions, I find you cannot do so due to either faults in the software directly or requirements/design issues that even if coded correctly do not allow an applicant to properly complete the process. This is a very small list of ones I have experienced.

- Required Account Creation/Login Issues.
- Force unreasonable passwords. Not provide the format required.
- Failure to send the password when asked by the applicant; telling them to come back in 5 minutes and ask again if not received is not quality.

- Forced to set up an account BUT still must resubmit most of the information each time you apply (sometimes 15-30 minutes of duplication).
- Allowed resume & support materials file types/sizes too small.
- Required fields that cause problems (so, so many different ways).
- Required fields not marked as required per the questions and do not require an answer but if left blank stops the application later.
- Fancy interconnected data entry dialog boxes (I have seen over 8) versus simple entry AND then have no way to save it – the save button is disabled after the first entry is selected.
- Forcing the user to change their artifacts for common fields, e.g., not send a resume if it has a 9 digit ZIP code (deliberate design issue) and the user must delete all 9 digit zip codes from their materials, e.g., DOC and PDF files.
- Applicant clicks on specific job description and is taken to the organizations web site … trouble is the specific description is lost. Applicant is expected to search for it again. In one I follow, the organization is national, has 6 "divisions," and lists up to a few hundred positions … if you didn't make specific note of the **exact** details of the position you could spend 30 minutes or more trying to find it again to apply …

- Or, click on the link and it takes you to a different job ad entirely.

Remember this is just a small composite of the many types of issues I run into in applying to positions – what a bad impression it makes for the organization!

## Besides the application process

The potential candidate's first impression of your organization is often the job ad they see.

**Do you consider that an applicant will even want to apply to your job ad?**

Consider what the applicant sees and must go through to apply.

The job description:

- Long and hard to read position descriptions.
- "Kitchen Sink" position descriptions with sometimes dozens or even pages of job requirements, in mini-font or block form, for a standard IT role, many meaningless.
- And of course, the "hidden requirement" not listed but this alone will kill an application if not listed on the resume.
- One Very Specific Requirement in an ad of generic requirements on one tool and for a specific minimum number of years e.g., *REQUIRED: 2 years of experience working with Microsoft Team Foundation Server.*

There are several other tools out there that do almost the exact same things, and knowing one or more of them makes it fairly easy to learn this one. And, what is the company expecting the candidate to learn after the first 6 months to 1 year that they must have a minimum of two years?
Remember the "learn how to learn" discussion previously?

The application process:

- Previous salary history required. Is the company really looking for a candidate or just fishing for what are the market salaries at the time? "He who mentions a salary first loses" is a very well known phase. **And remember it is more than salary** - but you may be rejected immediately based on the number you provide! DON'T!!!
- Lengthy job application to just to submit a resume, I've seen up to 1-2 hours to complete, and most of the time the job applicant never hears back from the company anyway. Before the internet, you didn't spend 30-90 minutes or more until you at least got a response or an interview THEN you completed the actual application.
- References required as part of the online job application, this is hiring not application.

And one of my favorites...

- **Require an online screening "Pre-test" BUT <u>the test itself has errors</u>.** "Failing?" gets you an auto reply that you are not being considered! Wow! Only if I do it wrong, do I get a chance to tell them how to do it right! NO THANKS!

  BTY, this test came from the internet and had serious errors – do you want to work for a company like that? Do you trust everything you read/get on the internet?

- And the failure of even common courtesy:
  Failure to send any word of decline after an in-person interview Even in this "modern" age, not to send a thank you or decline "letter/email" after an in-person interview is still highly RUDE and inconsiderate.

## Agencies/Recruiters

In my email I have three folders for agencies/recruiters – NO, Maybe, and Work With.

Why don't I just delete the no's – because I don't want to forget they are just that, NO WAY!

• • •

**On the web your competator is just one click away... do it right or click and you are h-i-s-t-o-r-y.**

• • •

The Maybe group might get another chance to earn my attention – but only with real effort.

The Work With ones are the best and are the ones I work with and also refer.

One of the online job aggregators that I get numerous daily emails from lists a certain job website that has jobs in my field that I would love to apply to – easily.

Unfortunately, this website has two issues I dislike. First, it is a subscription only site, i.e., you must have signed up with them to apply to their listed jobs; OK, I signed up. Second, when I signed up they forced a password different from my standard job site password that I use. Ok, when that happens, and others do it as well, I just have them email me the password again.

Well, on this site, to get them to email you the new password, you have to supply the old password as a "security" measure! WHAT? So there is no way I can change the password. My other option is to sign up again using a different email address – na!

So I just ignore all the emails and jobs from that source. And by-the-way, I still get all the same job listings from several other sources!
There is a moral to this story, on the web your competator is just one click away...

do it right or click and you are h-i-s-t-o-r-y!

# Conclusion

If you don't get a 2nd chance to make a good 1st impression, how many organizations have lost highly qualified candidates because they could not even apply to the job ad?

How many outstanding QA professionals have chosen to not apply to your organization because they knew if the application process was this poor in quality what their everyday work experience would be like?

I am one for sure!

# Words of Wisdom

- Biggest problem with graduates is the "lack of ability to work as a **TEAM**."
  [Lourdes Ortiz – Speak To Win Conference February 20, 2016]

- In adult learning, you forget **90%** of what you learn in **30 days** unless you use it! The 10% is what I want to make sure my students remember – the real world stuff.

- NEVER let your ID be **ID 10 T**.

- Image is someone's **First Impression** of you and what others take away about you is your **Reputation**.

- You always **Praise** in Public and Criticize in **Private**.

- When it comes to good staffing – It's the **QUALITY** not **QUANTITY**!

- It's not as important who you know as it is **WHO** knows **YOU**.

- How you do **ANYTHING** is how you do **EVERYTHING**. [Cindy Carpenter, Toastmasters Award Winning Speaker]

- For Sales/Interview/etc. A **good** Sales person/Interviewee etc. asks themselves on the way to the presentation "What am I going to **SAY**" while a **great** person asks themselves "What am I going to **ASK?**"

- HR (Human Resources) comes from the Latin Term "you don't get the job unless I **LIKE** you!" ☺ [Lourdes Ortiz – Speak To Win Conference February 20, 2016]

- You always take every interview you are offered; from each you learn something and become a better interviewee.

# Chapter Two

## ♣Leadership♣

• • •

**Management
is doing
things right…**

**Leadership is
doing the
right things…**

***Peter F.
Drucker***

• • •

and

• • •

**The most powerful
*Leadership* tool you
have is your own
personal example**

***John Wooden***

• • •

## A good leader knows their job is to...

1) **<u>Communicate</u>** (**# 1 job**)

2) Hire the right people (Hire Smartly) to follow their Direction in order to achieve their vision and goals....

3) Set the Vision & Mission with Goals & Direction to achieve them

4) Clear away obstacles

5) Get out of their way!

Without a leader who is engaged and most of all supportive, failure is the expected norm!

• • •

**A leader is never afraid to hire people <u>smarter than them</u> ... they want to be surrounded by smart people! Challenge invigorates a Leader!**

***Author Unknown***

• • •

## Success or Failure

Success or failure is determined by many factors, both external and internal.

External factors are not only the physical world itself but other people as well.

Internal factors can include: motivation, drive, and skill.

• • •

**Success or Failure triad:**

**Responsibility**

**Accountability**

**Authority**

• • •

But all other factors beging equal, the success or failure traingle will determine if you have the possibility of success or if you are doomed to failure.

NEVER allow yourself to be given the Responsibility or Accountability WITHOUT the Authority! The Authority is what gives you --- Ownership!

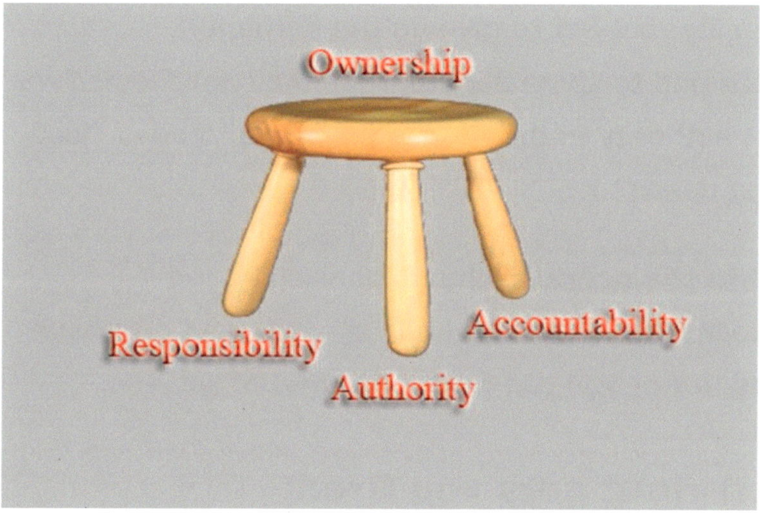


A manager will always give you the responsibility or accountability, **but a leader will also assign appropriate authority to get the job done right!**

**Responsibility**, it's on us! We all have been given the responsibility for something.

**Accountability**, we are not only held responsible, but it is "our head on the chopping block."

People will sometimes take responsibility for something but don't want to be held accountable if it fails; "it wasn't my fault, *{insert person, place, or thing}* prevented me from getting it done."

**Authority**, the usual reason for the above failure scenerio is the authority was not granted as well. People, e.g., managers, find it easy to give responsibility and accountability, but not to give up the authority! Sometimes and to some degree, they may not themselves have that authority to give up the authority needed (just gets worst doesn't it).

But, **within the scope** of the responsibility and accountability you are being held to, you **must** also have the **authority** or you can not be assured of success.

## Doing it right gets you fired!

Sometimes it is hard to tell if you have that authority or not?

I have always wanted to be able to follow this General's idea and do it right – <u>without</u> the being fired part.

I heard this story a long time ago and have no way to know if it is true – but it does sound like it would happen, so I believe it.

A two or three star Air Force General was assigned to head a very large, expensive development project. Being a good officer, he took his job seriously.

He went to his people and said "write me the User's Guide." So they worked with the customer and wrote the User's Guide. The customer was happy with how the software would work. They worked out the details, e.g., response times.
Next the General took the **approved & accepted** User's Guide and said "now, go build me this." They did...

The customer was happy, the project finished early, under budget, and met the customers expectations. **100% success!**

The General was fired, i.e., allowed to retire. He had not followed the "proper" development process!

**No good deed goes unpunshed.**

Why is it we have **90/50/50** project failure? Not hard to see!

## Words of Wisdom

- Decision by Indecision is a fallacy of **LOGIC**.

- A leader must be able to **Present** their ideas in a clear and concise manner to any person or group of people.

- A leader knows that **"you cannot, not communicate!"** Everything a leader does or says communicates something about who they are or what they want.

- A leader knows that people follow who they **Believe** in... not always who they agree with ...

- A leader knows that people follow who they **Trust** ... not always who they agree with ...
  and
- A leader knows that people follow who makes **them** feel good ... about **their** lives ... not the leaders...

- INTEGRITY: (academic for accreditation) and PERSONAL: Do what you say you will do!

- You must establish a GOAL, if you aim at nothing you hit it every time

  AND

- You don't fail in life because you set your goals "to high and miss" you fail because you set them "to low and hit them." [Brian Admas – Speak To Win Conference February 20, 2016]

- Failure is not the opposite of success, it is part of success [author unknown]; remember that the best homerun hitter in baseball also had the most strikeouts, but he never gave up and always hit for the homerun.

- Winners never quit and quitters never win. [author unknown]

- Management owns the process; don't blame the individual worker for a failure of the **process**.

- You **NEVER** surprise your boss! You always keep them up-to-date (to the level they require) and **ALWAYS** give them accurate, complete, and truthful information.

- If the first time an employee hears their performance is not meeting expectations is at their annual performance review, then the manager is **sub**standard at doing their job.

# Chapter Three

## ♣Project Management♣

**The THREE Measures of Project Success:**

**As agreed upon:**

**ON TIME:**

**ON BUDGET (Cost):**

**MEETS EXPECTATIONS (Requirements/Scope):**

• • •

**How does a large project become late – ONE day at a time!**

**AND when you fail on TIME, you automatically also fail on BUDGET ...**

• • •

As the PM, you only get to pick **two** qualities; the other is dictated by those two!

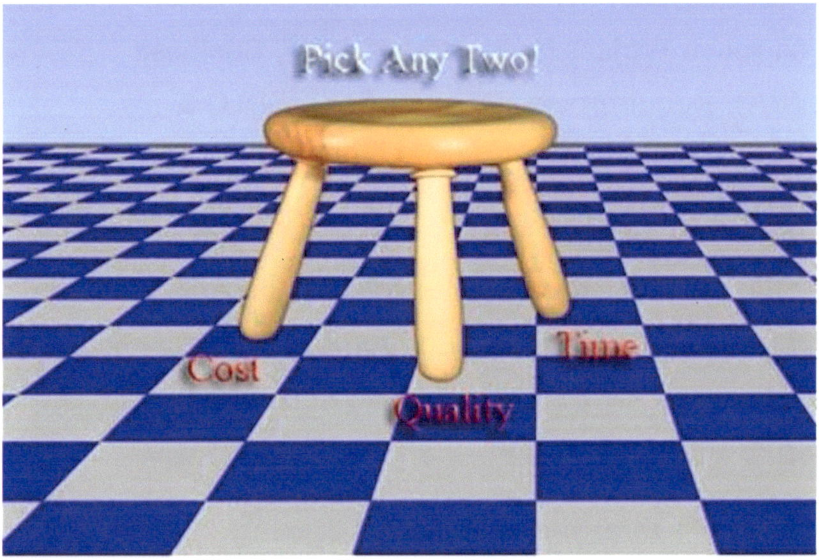


Or put another way....

Source unknown

## Introduction

While my titles usually had something to do with QA (Process & Software) my actual work and skill sets, include as much Project Management (PM), Business Analyst (BA), Requirements Analyst (RA), SDLC & methodology, and metrics, etc.

To me, these are all intertwinted and each required to do a proper job for any title. Even in a larger organization with separate teams for each title, you must do your job with the others in mind to help ensure quality is built in at each step of the process.

My Master's is in Information Systems **Management**; which includes the management of both projects (PM) **and** people; the systems piece is much easier☺

## Where do you start?

Let's start the PM part with a brief word on the SDLC because it helps define how the PM role will be implemented as opposed to defined; the actual definition of Project Management stays the same.

Most job ads I see for Project Managers include the SDLC or Methodology (A body of practices, procedures, and rules used by those who work in a discipline or engage in an inquiry; a set of working methods) as a requirement, i.e., experience in a specific one, usually incorrectly!

*See the SDLC chapter for more about the overall SDLC; if this is new to you jump to that chapter now to get an overview then come back for how it fits into Project Management.*

In more and more text books written by younger authors, I see what I consider to be a major mistake that gets carried over to what organizations are requiring and expecting for a PM position.

The System/Software Development Life Cycle is just what the name says it is! The SDLC just defines the stages/phases.

**The SDLC is the SDLC**.... And you have different methods (methodologies) to implement it. I group these into two basic groups: non-iterative (waterfall) and iterative, e.g., Agile.

So where do we start, hopefully with a Project Manager who knows the difference between the SDLC and the methodologies used to implement it – even if the organizations do not!

A good PM can adapt to and adopt the methodologies of the various development environments using the PM principles.

• • •

**Actions are the only useful outcome of process improvement**

**Sometimes knowing how things came about (came from) makes a difference!**

## Some Tidbits for Starters

I do not know the orginal source for these and credit the proper authors; but I find these too good to not pass along.

- Take chewable bites.
  - If you undertake too large a process change at one time, the team will likely choke on it.
- Love the small victories – you don't get too many big ones!
- Look for Allies – Cultivate, thank, and reward them.
- **Action Plans MUST turn into actions to be useful**. Actions are the only useful outcome of process improvements.
- Use gentle pressure – Relentlessly applied!
  - The only way forward is to keep the change initiative visible and to continually chip away at it.
- **Focus – Focus – Focus!**
  - Busy teams can only work on three, two, or maybe even only one process improvement initiative at a time. (also see CPI below)
  - **But never work on fewer than one** ☺

## Continuous Process Improvement

Continuous Process Improvement (CPI) is a key to being successful. In the business world, those that stand still are quickly run over... but CPI takes work!

With each change comes a learning curve - the Learning Curve is an **unavoidable** part of process improvement.

It takes time, money, and effort and often is given up on when the going gets tough; just when you must not give up!

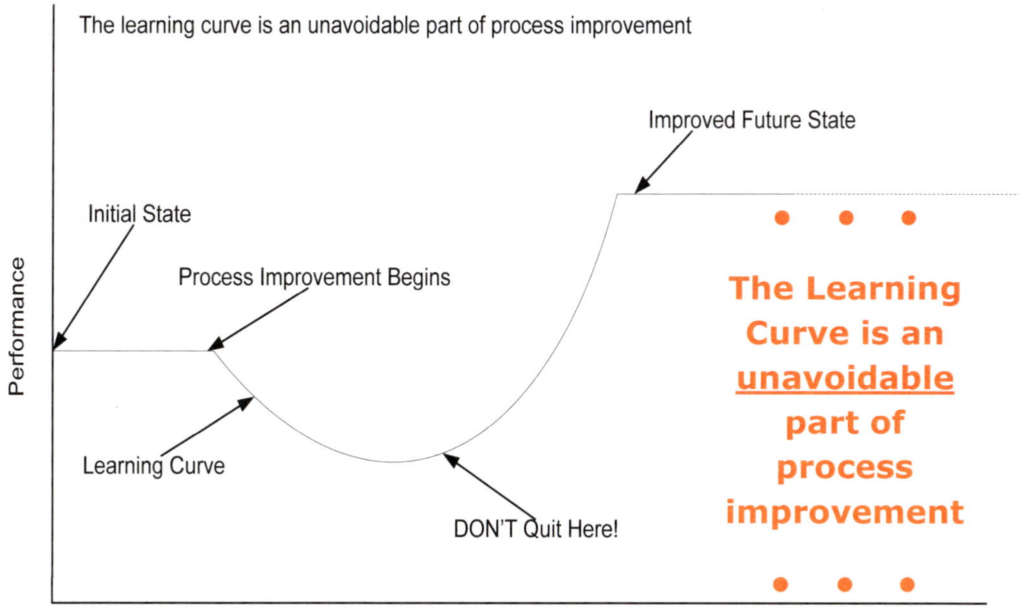

## Burdened Rate: What Is It?

What is a Burdened Rate? There are many answers and formulas used –

• • •

**Burdened Rate can help you budget better**

• • •

What works for you?

- The simplest (incorrect) formula is: What does it cost to keep the doors open per month divided by the number of employees. **AKA Burn Rate**.

– But this can be misleading when applied to specific development projects except for the small start-up that is all development related.

- **Better**: A fully burdened labor rate is an hourly labor rate that includes all of the **indirect** costs of providing a product/service, e.g., fringe benefits, overhead expenses, General & Administrative expenses, profit. It would **not** include travel and other direct costs.
- The PM cost factor to "do what you do" or "build what you build."

## Burdened Rate: What it is Not?

What is a Burdened Rate? Not the same as Burn Rate!

- The Burn Rate would include all the costs that Burdened Rate does not. Note: some elements will overlap both rates.
- Burn Rate: Keep the doors open… Always higher than Burdened Rate!

It is important to know what the Burdened Rate is and what it is for you; can be by company, division, department, group, team, function, etc.

Once determined (takes some work to create it), you can quickly and with a high degree of accuracy use it to help estimate project costs, i.e., budget or bid better; the budget/cost piece of **90/50/50**.

Plus once created you can use it without giving away your specific costs for the components, e.g., individual salaries.

## How Long Will It Take?

One of the most common questions I have been asked as the PM or QA is "how long will it take to….." complete the project, finish the requirements, test cases, run the tests, etc.

At each company I have worked for, I have created new and unique methods to answer these questions; most often using spreadsheets so I can use formulas to calculate the answers quickly from input data.

I have created spreadsheets to take the number of business requirements and calculate all the remaining key gates (checkpoints & artifacts) throughout the SDLC; an early calculation and refinement of the project length based on actual numbers versus the initial estimates (SWAG) – remember we are wrong <u>90%</u> of the time. I have created them to say how long it will take to create test cases and how long testing would actually take to run through the test cases (an interesting point here is that in its first use one spreadsheet was more accurate than both the QA manager and the most experienced Sr. QA Engineer. I have created them to track project trends based on scores of key elements that only took minutes to enter at any specific point/gate yet could then calculate the overall project status. And I have created them for anomaly tracking to answer the questions "when will testing be done?" or "where are we in the testing?"

• • •

**If you can't measure it, you can't manage it.**

• • •

I totally believe that "**if you can't measure it, you can't manage it**."
So I have created scores of different metrics tools, mostly in spreadsheets because I always have that tool if no others.

**And I am ALWAYS better than 90/50/50 when I am running the project and listened too.** (also, see Productivity below)

I take into all that I do, PM, QA, metrics, requirements, etc. the same determination and skills that as a developer, to my knowledge, no software that I wrote ever failed in production – a 100% success rate! And, yes, I did software development/engineering on some major zero tolerance applications like corporate taxes to the IRS and the Space Shuttle.

## Lessons Learned

Oh, so many books will at least give a sentence or two on the concept of doing a lessons learned file and presenting it at the end of the project in the Post-Mortem review. You do a Post-Mortem review, don't you?

Trouble is, is it after the project is over? Yes, it is nice to record what when wrong etc., but how often does that really get fed back to the next project or project manager?

I have always kept a lessons learned file, even before studying PM, as a way to do better myself. Even in aerospace with all the highly trained and educated folks, I was noted for actually doing it, "the only one to actually ever keep one."

**Lessons Learned: a PM life saver**

Most modern concepts of PM think in terms of itertive development versus a waterfall methodology. Well, itertive development means that each cycle is a mini-project. Therefore, you must keep the lessons learned file and do the Post-Mortem at the end of each cycle, not just an overall project one the end of project. Make it a living, ongoing and useful artifact.

I was able to do this in a unique way to fit the specific environment I was in. When I was put into my role, we were doing sometimes five or more quick installs per day to fix the issues from the last install; I was eventually able to take that to two planned installs per week.

One of the methods I used to do that was to turn my lessons learned file into the "gotta list." Whatever issues that got into **production** were analyzed and the root cause determined. The cause was added to the "gotta list" and the next release could not go into production until every item on the list was signed off by the developer(s) that it had been checked for and passed testing – the same mistake was not to be made twice! The list was of course ever growing so developers hated having to verify each item everytime, so they worked harder to not add to the list. **Work smarter not harder!**

And it was a trackable metric and a source of pride to not add to the list in your install(s).

So what happened here? We did some CPI (continuous process improvement), lessons learned, regression testing, quality & schedule & cost improvement, and developer buy in to the process, all with one tool.

## Productivity

90/50/50
or is it really
2.5%

I want to end this chapter on a very important topic for Project Management.

In The Problem section I introduce the concept of **90/50/50**. There are far, far too many reasons for this book to cover to explain how we get to this state. See The Problem for an overview and a look at the 50% (not meeting expectations) and also the CoQ chapter to help explain the 50% (over budget).

**Which leaves for here the 90% ... we are very, very bad at scheduling projects!** There are a number of reasons why, but I want to talk about just one of them.

Think of this ... how long would any PM or manager keep their job if when given an assignment they were honest with their boss and said something like:

> Thanks for the project and, oh, by the way, just so you are aware upfront, I have about a 2.5% chance of being fully successful ... this includes a 90% chance the project will be late, a 50% chance it will go over budget, and a 50% chance it will not meet customer expectations!

I personally have never met a boss that accepted that bit of honesty – have you?

But that IS the reality! Why, oh why, would anyone want this job? ☺

Let's discuss just one view of the reason for the 90% - **personnel scheduling**; remembering that there are many other types of scheduling that goes into PM as well.

**Productivity and 8 Hours per Day?**

When you plan your project schedules – how many hours per day do you expect from each project member to meet the deadline?

- 8 hours per day is the default standard and the "normal" work schedule.
- But of course – you are an experienced PM and know not to use 8 because of bathroom breaks etc. So you use 7 hours day!
- And of course your dedicated folks will work overtime and be more productive – right?

**Sorry – WRONG!**

One aerospace study found an individual is only productive 25% to 35% per day. This is only 2 to 2.8 hours per day – 10 to 14 hours per week.

- But then we all know aerospace is not productive – right? Doesn't mean the studies are wrong! Depends on many study factors not known.
- A commercial industry study (reported by SQE) found productivity of 4 to 5 hours per day – 20 to 25 hours per week. Only a little better but again what are the study metrics based on?

- Working doesn't mean Productivity … And it is more than just focusing on your task(s) without interruption or getting something "done."
- Is it productive if the work is incomplete or poor quality and must be redone later? (see the CoQ chapter)

For the studies above, I do not know the methodology used, so I can't repeat these studies to verify the results.

From my actual working experience I fully believe they are correct!

But being the over-achiever I am, I wanted to find a way to verify the numbers themselves with a methodology I did understand. And as luck would have it, in an "earlier" (pre-IT) life, I had experience with a totally difference concept of looking at productivity throughout the day – human biological cycles.

There are many cycles in nature and humans. The one that would apply directly here is our daily 90 minute cycles (ultradian rhythm). Each 90 minutes we go through a cycle where for 45 minutes we are on an up mode with our concentration and abilities increasing and then 45 minutes were our skills are decreasing, a down cycle, where we can't focus as well, are more easily distracted, etc.

I mapped these cycles into the work day and came up with the following results:

## Another Way to look at Productivity

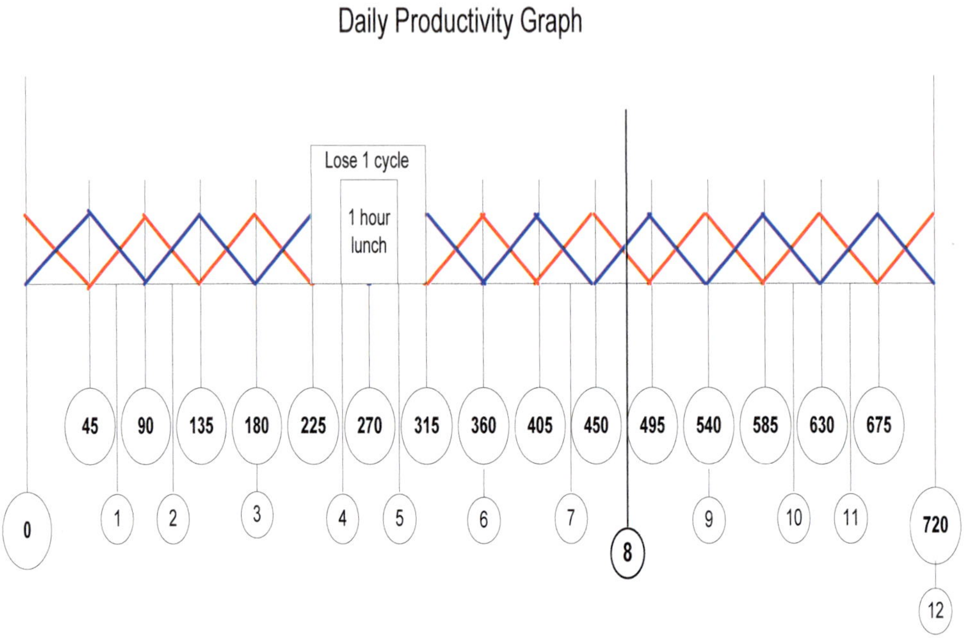


As to productivity:

- 90 minute cycles = 45 min up & 45 min down
- 480 minutes = 8 hours / 90 minutes = 5.33 cycles per day
- 4.25 (45 minute) UP cycles per day
- 4.25 * 45 minutes each cycle = 191.25 minutes per day = 3.18 productive hours per day = 16 hours per week (with only 1 interruption (lunch) per day)

These results are within the average of the aerospace and SQE studies (3 to 3.9)! And this time we know the basis of the metric – sounds like possible independent verification of the numbers? Taken together as a trend line for project planning and compared to your specific metrics, you should be able to focus on areas of improvement.

## So How Do I Plan My Projects?

So how many hours per day should I use for project planning?

- 8 is too high – so does 7 work better? How about at least 6 hours?
- 5 hours per day – "I can't afford that much time for this project!"
- And for sure 2 to 4 hours per day is IMPOSSIBLE!!!
  **Note: The average of the three studies is only 3.36 hours per day.**
- And of course, all numbers must include team members being at work.
  - You must account for holidays, vacations, sick days, other days off.
  - And at work: company meetings, phone calls, etc. etc.

**Well then how many hours per day should I use for project planning?**
Well my experience is that for:

- Short term projects (< 6 months) you can use 6 hours per day as an average **IF** you can expect some overtime at the expected "crunch times" at the end of delivery cycles **AND you have a good development process in place**.
- Long term projects (6 months or more) you should use no more than 5 hours per day – again **IF** you can expect some overtime at the expected "crunch times" at the end of delivery cycles **AND you have a good development process in place.**

This of course, is only for **initial project planning and you must refine and redo the numbers as the project moves forward** ... expect that it will take longer than originally planned IF you expect to maintain QUALITY.

## Conclusion

I have only touched on a very few of the many lessons I have learned over the years.

I have also condensed and left out other information regarding human cycles that can also have an effect on productivity to focus on just one aspect. Nothing having to do with Project Management is as simple as these topics imply.

• • •

**So many issues – so few pages ☺**

• • •

# Chapter Four

## ♣Metrics♣

• • •

**If you can't measure it … you can't management it!**

***Original source unknown***

• • •

You are not lost if you don't know where you are going.

You are lost if you don't know where you are **NOW**!

**Metrics** tell you where you are now.

## Introduction

I love spreadsheets! Spreadsheets are so good for tracking metrics and they are cheap in that we already have them available. You can even use them to do trend analysis plus produce charts and graphs.

• • •

**If I plan to track it or do it more than once – it goes into a spreadsheet!**

• • •

I am a firm believer in management by measurement. Yes, sometimes gut feel is also important, but you are not lost if you do not know where you are going or how to get there ...

You are lost if you don't know where you are now ... and metrics tell you where you are now!

## The Joy of Spreadsheets

Like I said above, I love spreadsheets and I have created hundreds over my career for both work and home. I use at least 20 or so at home on a regular basis to track all measurable aspects of my financies, job offers, birthdays, lists of many types, etc. etc. etc. I use a spreadsheet like many folks use Word, because I can do text but many others things as well, like sorting. And I never know when I want to add some sort of date calculations.

For work, I have used spreadsheets to create every artifact needed to run projects! And I can even do charts. It's also nice to have a charting tool, one to do presentations, and an easy diagraming one like Viso, but they are not required to run a project.

Other tools may have additional features and do things faster or easier … but if money for tools is an issue, I can do "old school" with Word and Excel; **and do it right!**

I even used Excel and VBA (self taught) once to automate creating all the spreadsheets (reports) that a company used on a weekly and monthly basis. Something that had taken six people, including one very expensive senior analyst, working full time to do previously.

But what does this have to do with metrics? Spreadsheets are great for also keeping metrics on the cheap.

## Trend Analysis

Data points alone do not allow you to manage your project, no matter how many there are. Too many just make it impossible for the human to make meaningful sense of them.
But, if you can run a trend line through the data points you can start of make sense of where you are and as stated above then start to find your way forward.

• • •

**Humans can only manage 7 +/- 2 things at one time.**

***Source unknown***

• • •

**Management by measurement** is about the **smart** use of the data.

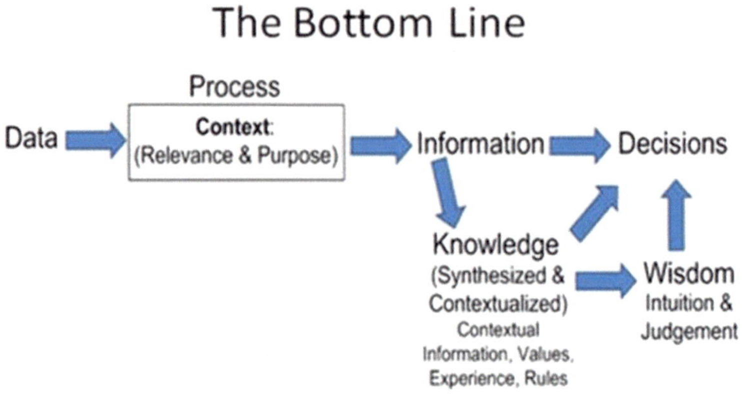


The smart use of the data is not to use it until it has been processed into information – it is from the **information** we make decisions – not the raw data. In other words, from the data develop the trend line(s) which are the information you use to make decisions.

## Conclusion

There are many, many ways to collect data, spreadsheets, databases (dah!), paper & pencile, graphs and charts, etc. I use spreadsheets because they are easy, available, and fast to use.

I have even used a spreadsheet to create a Decision Support System using a crude Expert System Inference engine (an example in my Management Information Systems class). It used actual data from the past to help predict what to do in the future.

I cannot detail here all the ways I used metrics in the past and the ways I captured and presented the data and information.

My purpose is therefore just to get you thinking about the topic and what you can do with metrics and some ways to do it. Once you see the value of good metrics usage, you can go from there and improve your skills.

A key note is to only collect the data and metrics you plan to actually use. Do not overburden yourself, your staff, or others with the time or engery needed to collect data and produce metrics that you do not plan to use – just to say you have it! A few rounds of extra, meaningless and unused work and you will get no reply from your requests for the data or metrics, or worst, you will get meaningless feedback just to produce something, i.e., to check that off my task list.

With no data or metrics, hopefully you will withhold making assumptions – remember what to "assume" means .... But also be aware that ....

**BAD data is WORST than no data at all!!! GIGO.....**

# Chapter Five

## ♣Cost of Quality (CoQ)♣

## Introduction

BEFORE reading this chapter, take a minute and write down your definition for the cost of quality.

**"We don't have time/money to do THAT! We will fix it later!"**

The most common one I hear is, what it costs to make a quality product or provide a quality service, e.g., testing, having and following a process, using expensive "quality" parts, spending more time than you "have," or other definitions that translate to (less) time or (less) money than is really needed.

In other words "we don't have the time/money to do THAT! We will fix it/do it right later!"

**I am sorry to tell you – but all those are WRONG!**

Read on....

# Cost of Quality (CoQ)

CoQ is a term that's widely used – and widely misunderstood.

• • •

**CoQ: Actual Cost – perfect quality (1st time / every time)**

• • •

The "cost of quality" isn't the price of creating a quality product or service. It's the cost of NOT creating a quality product or service THE FIRST TIME.

The Cost of Quality is NOT the cost for QA, testing, qualified personal, a little extra time to get "it" right, or any of the other reasons given when you say "we don't have the time/money to do that!" How is it we never have time/money to do it "right" the first time but always have time/money to do it over? That is your CoQ!

In short, any cost that would not have been expended if quality were perfect contributes to the cost of quality.

The simple definition for CoQ is:

**Actual Cost – perfect quality (1st time/every time) = CoQ**

- Examples include:
- The reworking of code.
- The retesting of code (regression testing).
- The rebuilding of a tool.

- Everyday examples include:
- The correction of an incorrect bank statement.
- The reworking of a service, such as the replacement of a food order in a restaurant.

Quality Costs can be grouped into several types:

Prevention Costs

- The costs of all activities specifically designed to prevent poor quality in products or services.

Appraisal Costs

- The costs associated with **measuring, evaluating or auditing** products or services to assure conformance to quality standards and performance requirements.

Failure Costs

- The costs resulting from products or services not conforming to requirements or customer/user needs.

- Internal are costs occurring prior to delivery or shipment of the product or the furnishing of a service to the customer.

- External are costs occurring after delivery or shipment of the product and during or after furnishing of a service to the customer.

Total Quality Costs

• The total of all the costs.

This represents the difference between the actual cost of a product or service and what the reduced cost would be if there were no possibility of substandard service, failure of products or defects in their creation. Every time work is redone, the cost of quality increases.

## Real World CoQ

Four real world examples of companies that learned the meaning of CoQ the hard way...

The first was a computer **manufacturer** that had a sterling worldwide reputation for engineering quality; so much so that they didn't focus on QA and testing. This lack of Quality focus ended up with the sale of one (just one) bad server line. The loss of sales and reputation eventually ended up with them being bought out and closed down.

• • •

**I'm choosing four examples, and I am sure you have "billions" more .... I see them so many times a day.**

• • •

Second was a multinational hundred year old company that was a leader in several industries, consumer financial lending, insurance, etc. The company tried to combine their multiple local systems into one worldwide common system. After spending over $22 million dollars on the failed software project, the parent company sold them for the value of their customer base.

The above two examples show that the CoQ is often much more than just money; it can be reputation, the organizations very existence, and the loss of people's careers and income, etc.

While not forcing the organization out of business, one large telecom company was upgrading the software for their telephone switching equipment. A decision was made to not purchase a switch needed for operational testing at a cost of $50,000 dollars. When the software upgrade failed due to an unknown/untested defect, the system was down for a few hours. The loss to the company was in the **hundreds of millions of dollars** – due to the Service Level Agreements (SLA's) they had with their customers. What an expensive switch (decision) that turned out to be.

Or ask British Petroleum (BP) what the gulf coast oil spill CoQ is? In addition to all the actual costs of losing the oil rig, the lost oil, the environmental damage, the cost to the states, public, etc., you have the illnesses and <u>deaths</u> of wildlife and most importantly people, and the largest fine ever levied by the US government for a spill, 4.5 billion dollars; if only it really covered the actual, real costs involved☹

Especially as the last two examples above point out, the CoQ is measued in much more than dollars and cents of lost profit.

It is measured in the loss of careers and reputations, in damage to the environment, wildlife, and people! And even deaths!
Measured in ways we may not even know or can calculate. Measured in terms of years, maybe decades, and even generations!

• • •

**Quality is everyone's job and the cost of quality is paid by us ALL.**

• • •

# Part Two

## ♣Systems Development♣

The Guru of quality said it a long time ago...

● ● ●

**"Quality comes not from**
**inspection, but**
**improvement of the**
**development process."**

***W. Edward Deming***

● ● ●

# Chapter Six

## ♣Requirements♣

Requirements ARE:

• • •

**The single hardest and single most important part of any project!**

• • •

# Introduction

There must be thousands/millions or more pages on the Requirements topic. I will focus on listing some of what I see as the biggest issues of quality and briefly detail only a very, very few of what I think are most important or misunderstood. **I probability have more I could say on this subject than any other since requirements = quality or not!**

In my course on "IT Project Management" I get to barely touch on this topic, along with QA in general. Many of the topics I discuss deserve to be their own course as part of a degree in quality assurance. I try to impart a very few of these **hard learned** lessons in each course I teach.

## Requirements are...

**The single most important and the hardest thing to do in any project!**

Seventy to eighty/eighty-five percent or more of all anomalies come from the requirements and the resulting design. (also see Anomalies (Not Bugs) in Quality Assurance chapter)

• • •

**Requirements are: the single most important and the hardest thing to do in any project.**

**And quality requirements are even harder than that!**

• • •

Only about ten to fifteen percent are from the actual coding of software. But that is where all the attention and money is (mis)spent to "create quality."

Why not focus on what produces the "biggest bang for the buck?" Just doesn't seem to happen that often.

Why? That is the question I have never gotten a real answer to – oh, I have gotten a lot of answers but none that deal with the reality of the numbers.

## By The Numbers (Again)

As I stated in The Problem,

- 90% of all IT projects are delivered late (Aberdeen)
- 50% of all IT projects are delivered over budget (Gartner)
- 50% of all IT projects fail to meet business objectives (Gartner)

• • •

**90/50/50 or is it really a 2.5% success rate**

• • •

I start my classes with this information ... and I refer to **90/50/50** all throughout the course whenever I am discussing why quality is lacking; this is every class because there is no shortage of reasons.

What Typically Goes Wrong in Software Projects?

- Scope Creep [requirements - Be realistic: assume that if a requirement can be misinterpreted, it will be misinterpreted.]
- Business requirements continuously reopened
- Requirements not traced through development process
- Cutting testing efforts: development milestones take precedence
- Unexpected performance and data issues
- Defects in critical business scenarios before go-live

**Gartner:**
http://www.entovation.com/seminars/SelingerBTO.pdf

**Aberdeen:**
http://www.think-ebiz.com/2012/03/why-do-web-projects-fail.html

**Standish:**
http://www.zdnet.com/blog/projectfailures/new-it-project-failure-metrics-is-standish-wrong/513

Note that none of these reasons have to do with the actual coding of software!

One discusses testing (correctly) but ignores the point that testing is a backend component of QA; one that proper QA reduces. And the other is related to the Design phase (if not directly to requirments) – the design coming directly from the requirments (70% requirements & 10-15% design – directly from the requirements good or bad).

The bottom line is – to fix the problem(s) you **fix the front-end** not keep redoing the backend (CoQ)!

And in most small to medium size organizations, this falls to QA - if allowed. In my career in QA, I have performed the PM/BA/RA/Metrics/etc. roles as often as the QA one – as part of it.

**You can't do proper QA without doing these properly as well**.

• • •

**It is up to 200 times more expensive to fix a requirements defect in production than in the requirements phase.**

• • •

## The Cost

If the problems come from the requirements but we don't do them correctly or fix them in the requirements phase ....

We get the 90 in part from rework and the 50/50 directly from the requirements:

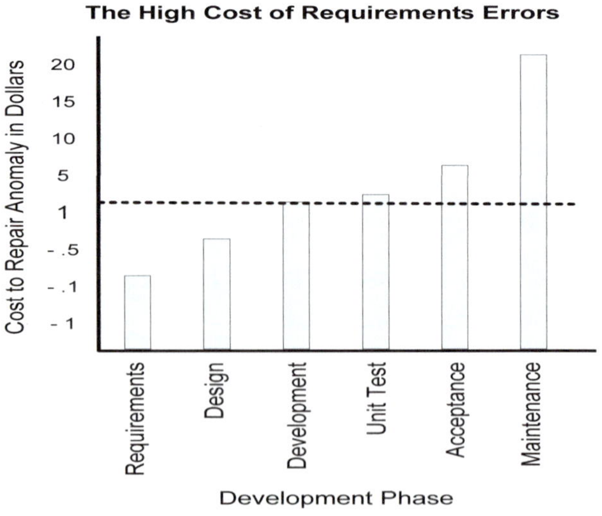

# A Big part of the Problem

As I teach in my classes, one of the biggest problems I see that leads to poor requirements is the simple misunderstanding of **And** versus **Or**. This is true in everyday life as well. But when it comes to computers it is **CRITICAL!**

• • •

**AND vs. OR**

**a critical difference**

• • •

The truth table below shows the difference between AND & OR (for this book you can ignore the XOR, but it IS important for computers).

| Truth Table | | | |
|---|---|---|---|
| T (p) | AND / OR / XOR | F (q) | = |
| T | AND | T | T |
| T | AND | F | F |
| F | AND | T | F |
| F | AND | F | F |
| | | | |
| T | OR | T | T |
| T | OR | F | T |
| F | OR | T | T |
| F | OR | F | F |
| | | | |
| T | XOR | T | F |
| T | XOR | F | T |
| F | XOR | T | T |
| F | XOR | F | F |
| Warning: Different Computers/Applications program this differently | | | |
| Sometimes both sides are evaluated and sometimes not if the answer is known | | | |

For AND, <u>all</u> must be true for the equation to be true.

For OR, <u>all</u> must be false for the equation to be false.

In writing (English) a comma acts like an OR, e.g., in the sentence "I want to be **rich**, **loved**, **honored**, or **respected**" any one or all makes it a TRUE statement; and only FALSE if you do NOT want to be any of them.

And to compound the problem, writers will throw in a "and/or" construct "I want to be **rich**, **loved**, **honored**, and/or **respected.**"

Now what is the correct answer? Often times at a business level, the context of the sentence makes it "clear" [the "clear if known" fallacy] what the expected answer is, i.e., I know I want to be one of these so it is true; but computers do not have the same human concepts and don't care about being any of them. And when it is programmed the context is lost and the computer canNOT make human sense out of it. And really does the human either?

**Remember computers are binary machines and only know two states.**

Sentence one is clear as to the answer – you have only two possibilities:

| **rich** | **loved** | **honored** | **OR** | **respected** | **RESULTS** |
|---|---|---|---|---|---|
| T/F | T/F | T/F | OR | T | TRUE |
| F | F | F | OR | F | FALSE |

Sentence two is NOT clear as to the answer:

| **rich** | **loved** | **honored** | **AND/OR** | **respected** | **RESULTS** |
|---|---|---|---|---|---|
| T/F | T/F | T/F | OR | T | TRUE |
| F | F | F | OR | F | FALSE |
| T/F | T/F | T/F | AND | T | **TRUE or FALSE** |
| T/F | T/F | T/F | AND | F | FALSE |

Before you go off writing to tell me that I am wrong and you still know the answer once you determine the values for the data fields (rich, etc.) – **this was NOT the point of the exercise.**

**When do you use the AND, and when do you use the OR? The computer does NOT know that!**

And, while it might be (maybe?) clear to the person writing the business (person level) requirements, it is not clear to the person later writing the functional (computer level) requirements and the design - where the most problems are introduced.

**In other words when you add the "and/or" the requirement becomes ambiguous and therefore NOT a valid requirement.**

Bottom line:

- Conjunctions like "and" and "or" or a series of items separated by commas in a requirement suggest that several requirements have been combined.
- Never use "and/or" or "etc." in a requirement statement.
- Never use "i.e." or "e.g." in a requirement statement. And using "etc." with either of these is functionally and denotatively incorrect as well.

## A Real World Example:

English is an ambiguous language when we write it at the business level.

What is the correct answer?

"**Variable shall equal one-half of two plus two**"

How written ...
V = (2 divided by 2) + 2 >>> (½ of 2) + 2 = 3

**AND**

V = (2 + 2) divided by 2 >>> ½ of (2 + 2) = 2

This was actually part of the UNIX core O/S (Kernel) and different implementations of the O/S handled it differently which gave different results at the basic O/S level, e.g., system timings.

This affected the way the O/S itself worked, and therefore ALL applications running on the machine.

It took years to figure out and no telling how long to resolve ....

**Poor Users** ☹

## And then we make it WORST

Not only do we have the English problem – but we the have the human filters problem – or why a picture is worth a thousand words.

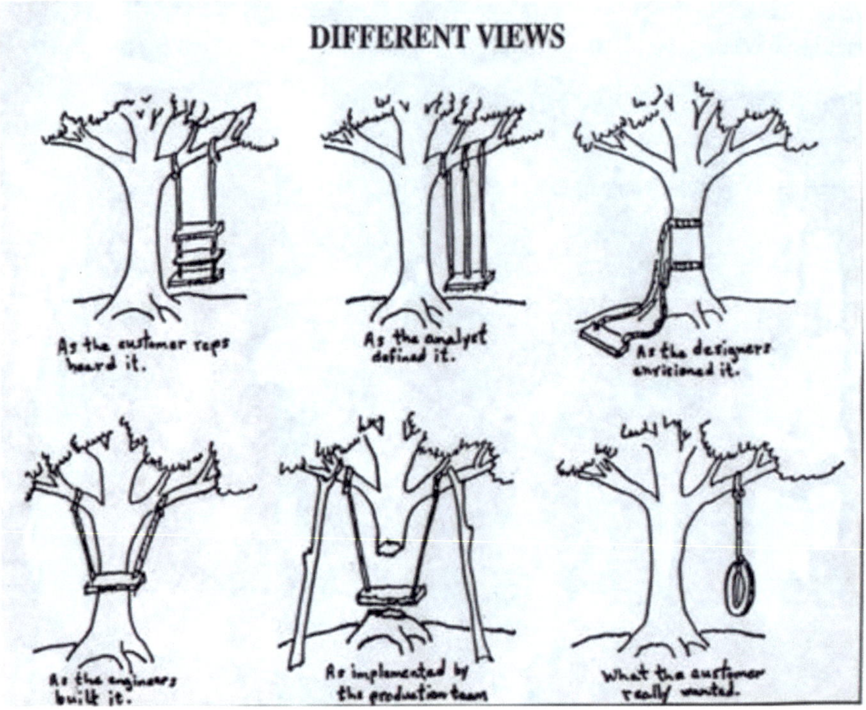


## A Good Start

Not only do we have the problems defining the actual functional requirements using English, then we have the fact that Quality is a collection of "ilities," the non-functional requirements, both internal and external.

There are somewhere around thirty-one or so of these qualities, not all of which actually end in "ilities."

Many years ago I wrote a short paper that proposes that for any organization at a SEI CMMI level 1 to 3, if you completely adopt nine (9) of the key ones you will improve your requirements process by **at least 100 percent**.

**Think CRUD – I always ask "did you CRUD that?"**

- Complete
- Correct (may be testable with only minor incorrectness, e.g., spelling errors)
- Unambiguous
- Consistent (with other individual requirements and across groups of requirements)
- Non-compound
- Verifiable
- Traceable
- Free of unwarranted design detail
- Modifiable

## Conclusion

I have only touched on a few of the so very many issues related to requirements. My goal here was just to tease you ...

# Chapter Seven

## ♣System/Software Development Lifecycle (SDLC)♣

## The Basic Concept

In the Project Management chapter I introduced this concept that I consider so important I start this chapter with it as well.

This is just such a common issue!

**Agile is not the SDLC – alternative or otherwise**

In more and more text books written by younger authors, I see what I consider to be a major mistake and this gets carried over to what organizations think the SDLC is.

The System/Software Development Life Cycle is just what the name says it is! In human life cycle terms think: conception (planning), development (construction), birth (release), execution (life), and retirement/death.

There are commonalities in how this happens for all humans, but the actual implementation (methodology) can be different. The same is true for projects. The SDLC just defines the Procedure / process and stages (I over simplify).

Agile is **not** the SDLC, it is **only one way** to implement the SDLC! The SDLC is **not** the "traditional" water fall method and Agile (Scrum, Pairs, Extreme, etc.) is **not** the "alternative" development process!

The SDLC is the SDLC.... And you have different methods (methodologies) to implement it (see **Basic Definitions** Below).

I group these into two basic groups: non-iterative (e.g., waterfall) and iterative.

Waterfall is the traditional development **method** and from it have emerged many variations. Agile is just one of these variations (iterative methods) with its own set of rules.

## Start With This

Whichever methodology you choose to implement the SDLC, I recommend you start with studying the Carnegie Mellon® Software Engineering Institute (SEI) and the **Capability Maturity Model Integration** (**CMMI**).

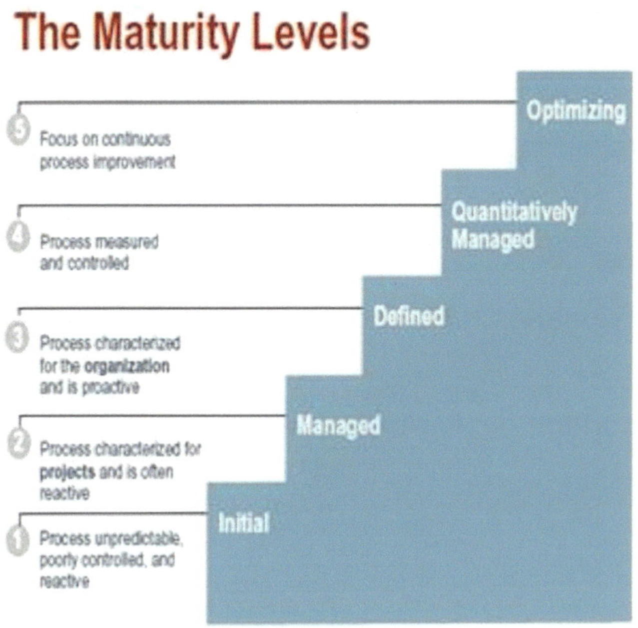


"… There is a strong correlation between the quality of the process used to develop software and the resulting software product"

*Software Engineering Institute*

The more you understand about this model and what it means the better you will be at everything else you will do in the development process.

## Basic Definitions

**PROCEDURE:**

A series of **actions** conducted in a **certain order or manner**: http://www.oxforddictionaries.com/us/definition/american_english/procedure#procedure__4

**PROCESS:**

A series of **actions or steps [or events performed to make something]** taken in order to achieve a particular end.

synonyms: **Procedure**

http://www.oxforddictionaries.com/us/definition/american_english/process

http://dictionary.cambridge.org/us/dictionary/american-english/process

**METHOD:**

A **particular form of procedure** for accomplishing or approaching something, especially a systemic or established one.

**METHODOLOGY:**

A system of **methods** used in a particular area of study or activity.

So the primary function of a software **process** is to determine the *order of the stages* involved in software development and to establish the *transition criteria* for going from one stage to the next. On the other hand a software **method** (methodology) primarily focuses on how to navigate through each phase.

**SO:**

SDLC stands for Systems/Software Development Life Cycle [AKA the Systems Development Process]. A Software Development Life Cycle is essentially a series of steps, or phases [see Procedure/Process above], that provide a model for the development and lifecycle management of an application or piece of software.
https://www.google.com/?gws_rd=ssl#q=SDLC

**THUS:**

The SDLC is a **Procedure/Process.**

**SO WHAT:**

Different authors, texts, writings lately tend to describe "Waterfall" as the Traditional SDLC and others, for example, **Agile** as the "Alternative" SDLC.

I think this gives the reader a false picture of what the SDLC really is. If you look at the definition of **Method**, you will see that each of many discussed approaches, e.g., Waterfall, Modified Waterfall (RUP), Cyclic, Agile, Object Oriented, SCRUM, Pairs Programming, Individual Development, XP, NASA, DOD, and on & on, are really a **METHOD** (particular form of procedure) NOT the Procedure, i.e., SDLC. And to say that only one (Waterfall) is the traditional one misses the point that many others have been around well before Agile etc.

In addition, each and every one of these "methods" with only slight variations follows the same basic "series of **actions or steps**."

1. Need Analysis & Definition
2. Investigation
3. Requirement gathering and analysis
4. Design
5. Construction [implementation or coding]
6. Integration & Testing
7. Implementation [deployment & maintenance]
8. Retirement

Of course there are many supporting activities to these basic steps. I am only trying to convey the top most concepts.

## SO WHAT AM I SAYING?

Simply that the SDLC IS the SDLC, the Life Cycle. There are not different SDLC's, but different **methods** to implement the SDLC.

In this way of thinking it is easier for everyone to share a common vision of the development cycle and the goals.

Each method is more alike than different, but various authors do not convey that well.

I was taught and propose that we see the SDLC as the Over-Arching (top-level) single life cycle. Under that we have two basic approaches: **non-Iterative** and **Iterative**.

Waterfall then is a **non-Iterative** method of the SDLC **not** the "Traditional SDLC." Most/all of the others listed are Iterative methods. Agile is only one of them, not the definition of the Iterative methods as it seems to me some authors are portraying it to be.

In picture form this looks like this:

**SOFTWARE DEVELOPMENT LIFE CYCLE (SDLC)**

| **Non-ITERATIVE** | **ITERATIVE** |
| --- | --- |
| Waterfall | Modified Waterfall |
| ... | Cyclic |
| | Agile |
| | ... |

The analogy I use is the human development life cycle (HDLC): conception, birth, life and care, and death. There are multiple methods of conception ("traditional," In vitro, surrogate, cloning) and multiple methods of birth ("natural", C-Section), many different methods of "development," and retirement (natural death, accident, murder).

But we do not call each different one a different HDLC – we think of each as different methods of the same "procedure."

**This is MY personal perspective on the issue; I am open to debate and discussion if you see it differently.**

## Words of Wisdom

- When considering an IT/IS system, always consider **SOFTWARE** before **HARDWARE**.
- All **PROTOTYPES** must be **THROWAWAY**.
- 70% of the Life Cycle cost of a system is in the **MAINTENANCE** phase.

# Part Three

## ♣Quality Assurance♣

Both Art and Science

**My personal logo to define QA**

## "QA in the Real World: My View from the Trenches"

A "Cliff Notes" guide to some basic Quality Assurance realities.

• • •

**If we build the most technically perfect product possible BUT the customer doesn't or can't use it – what have we really accomplished?**

• • •

This was the title for my original eBook series which started with the Quality Assurance chapters, and the other chapters grew from there. I debated long and hard about making it the first chapter in the book as well.
I went ahead and put it in the more traditional location at the end of the SDLC, not because as most authors do I see QA as "testing" that happens only after development – **SO WRONG,** but because I want to impress on the reader how bad we are at what we do and some of the reasons and ways we fail so badly.

And therefore, **how important QA is from the <u>very beginning</u>**!

QA starts with the first team members hired and with every meeting or activity thereafter. It helps in all aspects of the organization as the team dedicated to quality first & foremost throughout the whole organization.

**Do it once, do it right, and don't do it again!**

## 2 Slides that say a lot about being in QA

I begin all my "Brown Bag Lunch" on-the-job (OJT) presentations with this slide.

I tell my audience that the real message of this slide is that everyone will see, hear, and understand the same information differently (our unique filters) but since QA is at the heart of the SDLC, you must use the skill of **active** listening and your **skills in requirements analysis** to be sure the product or service meets the goal of customer satification, i.e., you are the customers representative in the development organization.

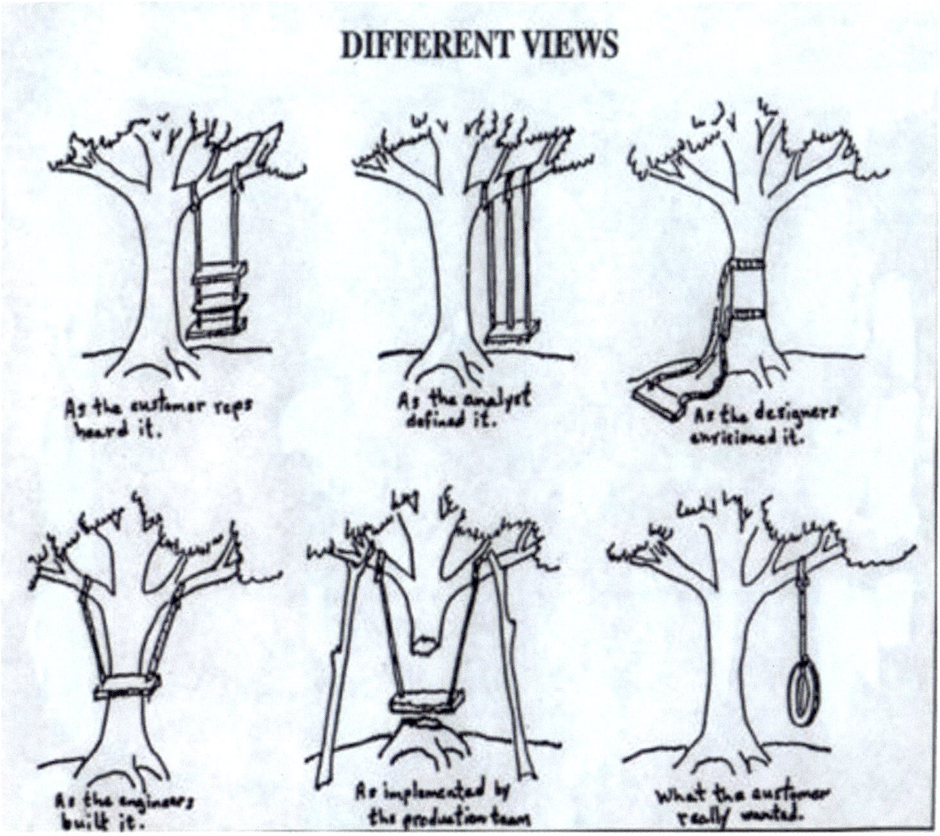

I conclude all my presentations with this slide.

In QA, a very thick skin and the tenacity to never give up, even under what can be tremendous pressure is a key to success.

"Political reality" so often prevents you from doing the job you know how to do correctly or requires a compromise in quality standards, **but the real failure is when you give up!**

# Chapter Eight

## ♣Quality Assurance♣

# Let's Start at the Beginning

## Where is QA Involved?

From the very beginning of the project – a quality product starts with a quality process.

Remember, **GIGO** (garbage in, garbage out).

Just starting a new organization? What is the foundation core team for quality?

The initial core group:

- Architect (may be the Entrepreneur),
- HR/Accounting,
- Quality Assurance (QA),
- Database guru, and
- Lead software engineer.

• • •

**Oh Yea, and pay the QA person the same as the DBA & software engineer.**

• • •

Oh Yea, and pay the QA person the same as the DBA & software engineer. WOW! Am I ever the idiot… who would ever do that, pay QA (a "tester") the same as the DB and software engineers – to do testing!

**OK, time to fold up shop and move onto the next "great" idea of yours – this one is over already!**

You do **not** know what QA is or what it does for your company, and most of all what it saves the company in time and money. (see the cost of quality (COQ) chapter)

I didn't say to hire a tester and pay them the same... hire a true QA professional.

Other than you, the Entrepreneur, which of the others above need the following range of skills?

1) Business and technical knowledge and experience; the interface between the technical and your customer/client.

2) Development / programming experience.

3) Knowledge of the various platforms & environments used.

4) As you develop your database, the ability and knowledge to develop a validation list for all variables to be used, e.g., type, minimum, maximum, length, format, data source, calculated or input. Proper validation & verification is then developed from the start.

5) Multi-trained **in several disciplines** including Project Management.

6) Technical knowledge, requirements writing, dual "language" ability (technical & user), and a fair degree of writing skill, like a technical writer.

7) Excellent analytical, troubleshooting, and problem solving skills.

8) The QA team is usually "the" process team as well or works with that team and must have process, methodology,

and metrics skills. And who will create your SDLC? Run the CCB (you have one of these, right)?

9) Management experience to become the manager of the QA team going forward.

10) And, they must still have all the skills and talents required to actually test products.

While each of the others has a single focus, it is your QA person that will **tie it all together with QUALITY and the customer in mind.**

## Anomalies (NOT Bugs)

When All Else Fails ...

A logo I had made up for one of my QA teams ....

**All bugs are anomalies, but not all anomalies are bugs**

**S**ystem / **S**oftware **A**nomaly **R**eport (SAR), my term for what most folks call a bug report. I only kind of agree to use the term bug for a coding error ... and this comes from how the term was first coined in the computer world.

Bugs are also often called by other names as well, e.g., defects, discrepancies, errors, issues. Discrepancy is the next closest to my preferred term Anomaly and my compromise term when some folks just will not accept Anomaly. But if you research the meaning of all of these and really consider what is being discussed, anomaly is the most correct term.

And....

Which sounds less threatening and more neutral? "Let's discuss the Discrepancies" or "Let's discuss the Anomalies." The first is like bug, error, defect, it immediately brings up a defensive attitude; anomaly doesn't tend to do that. **And sometimes the role of QA is as much about Psychology and Sociology as it is about computers.**

An Anomaly is a *"variance from an approved attribute"* (a difference from an agreed upon standard or requirement and the actual product itself). **This may or may not be a bug or defect** ... hence the use of the term. **Anomaly tracking is one of the most critical components of the software development and quality assurance efforts.**

When implemented well, Anomaly tracking greatly reduces overall project costs and improves schedule performance.

• • •

**If you don't build Quality in – you will be "SARry" later**

**You will find yourself testing the pieces after the fact.**

• • •

I have said elsewhere that you cannot test in quality!

But typically, testers receive a low-quality product at the tail end of development when there is tremendous pressure to deliver, even if the software is plagued with anomalies, i.e., defects, bugs, errors, or *variances from approved attributes*.

**The Goal is to:**
Build Quality In From The Start

**Because:**
You Can't Test In Quality

For early Anomaly detection and resolution to take place, Anomaly tracking and software development, i.e., SDLC, efforts should begin simultaneously. That is to say that Anomaly tracking begins with the first artifact of the SDLC.

**Anomaly tracking must be implemented throughout the SDLC**. This has been shown to lead to fewer released Anomalies.

And as a reminder, when it comes to those Anomaly Reports (aka "bugs") ...

A question QA gets from management every day is "how long will it take you ..." or "when will you be done ...." How do you answer this without anomaly tracking (also see metrics chapter)?
QA's answer is really all about one thing ... telling management what the Risk is of this choice versus that choice.

For all QA does, it boils down to being able to provide management with a Risk Assessment – pure and simple! It just takes a lot of work to make it a good one!

## Risk Management

Why is Anomaly tracking so important ... Risk Management!

And to management, Risk = Money!

The ranking of anomalies is based on two components: **Severity** and **Likelihood of Occurrence**. These two components combined provide a Deployment Risk measurement for the product not meeting expectations (Quality).

• • •

**Anomalies present a Risk in the product not meeting the expectations of the customer or end user of the product.**

• • •

### Risk

Risk is the term used to refer to the combination of the severity and the likelihood of occurrence of an anomaly. The risk factor can then be used as an input to a Change or Configuration Management (CM) function where unified, informed decisions can be made to set a priority for the anomaly or to determine criteria for release, e.g., Alpha, Beta or GA (release).

### Severity

Different organizations will use various levels and words to represent the same concept of the severity of an anomaly.

## Sample Definitions

Over my years in QA, I have developed a number of different versions of the severity charts below for different organizations based on their risk tolerance. The general format and design all come from my training in the RUP (Rational Unified Process). [now a division of IBM]

| Rank | Severity | Description |
|---|---|---|
| 1 | Urgent | a. Prevent the accomplishment of an essential capability, e.g., system crash, unrecoverable data loss.<br>b. Jeopardize personnel safety, business security, or other requirements designated "critical." |
| 2 | High | a. Adversely affect the accomplishment of an essential capability; **no** work-around solution is known.<br>b. Adversely affect technical, cost, or schedule risks to the project or to the life cycle support of the system; **no** work-around solution is known. |
| 3 | Medium | a. Adversely affect technical, cost, or schedule risks to the project or to the life cycle support of the system, but a work-around solution is known.<br>b. Impairment of critical system functions and workaround exists. |
| 4 | Low | a. Result in user/operator inconvenience or annoyance but does not affect a required essential capability.<br>b. Result in inconvenience or annoyance for development or support personnel, but does not prevent the accomplishment of those responsibilities.<br>c. Cosmetic issue |
| 5 | Enhancement | An enhancement or suggestion for improvement. |

Note: companies that use Rational tools often use severity names adapted from the Rational Unified Process (RUP), i.e., Critical vs. Urgent, Major vs. High, Average vs. Medium, Minor vs. Low. These are definable by the organization as long as the concept remains the same.

## Likelihood of Occurrence

The likelihood that a specific anomaly will occur is either:

- A known fact, i.e., happens every time the application is opened or a specific function or feature is triggered, or
- An educated guess based on the judgment of the R&D or QA Engineer, e.g., will occur every time but only in very specific or unusual circumstances.

The percent is only a reference to assist in judging the level to use and each percent is from the point given to the next higher level.

The following is a guide to determining this value

| Rank | Likelihood | Description |
|---|---|---|
| 1 | CERTAIN (100%) | Happens every time the user accesses the system, function, or feature in the normal course of usage. |
| 2 | HIGH (75%) | Happens in the normal course of usage on a frequent basis, e.g., several times during a normal usage cycle. |
| 3 | LIKELY (50%) | Happens in the normal course of usage on a regular basis, e.g., one time during a normal usage cycle. |
| 4 | LOW (25%) | Happens in the normal course of usage on a random basis, e.g., once every few days to a week such as doing a weekly status function. |
| 5 | OCCASIONAL (10%) | Happens only when a specific sequence of events occur that the user will not duplicate regularly, e.g., a setup function where an alternate course of action is available. |
| 6 | RARE (1%) | Happens only under specific and unusual circumstances outside of normal usage. This would also include random problems where a cause cannot be identified. |

## Priority Definitions

Companies may also define a set of rules to define when an **Anomaly** must be fixed (assuming **iterative** development is being used).

| Priority | Definition |
| --- | --- |
| "1" = Fatal | Must be fixed immediately.<br>There is no workaround or bypass available and testing cannot continue.<br>Defects that prevent further progress until resolved.<br>The entire application, or major component or function will not work. |
| "2" = Restricts ability to Test | Needs to be fixed in the next scheduled build.<br>There is a workaround or bypass available, and some testing can continue.<br>Defects that occur in a major function and are grossly incorrect.<br>Much of the functionality of this component is missing or does not function as expected.<br>Requirement on how a component is supposed to function is missing, vague or ambiguous. |
| "3" = Corrections prior to Alpha | The component tested does not perform as expected but testing can continue.<br>The component tested produces incomplete and inconsistent results.<br>Requirement regarding how a feature should be displayed (colour, font size, location) is missing, vague or ambiguous. |
| "4" = Corrections prior to Beta | The defect does not impair usability, and the desired processing results are obtained by working around the defect, e.g., highly visible typos will fall in this category. |
| "5" = Corrections prior to GA | The defect contains cosmetic anomalies, typos, unclear wording, or error messages in low visibility fields. |
| "6" = Post GA correction | Enhancements suggested by clients, developers, testers or others. |

## An Example

An example of likely combinations of severity and likelihood with the corresponding priority is shown below. Other combinations can be developed as required following this example and organizational polices.

**Risk = Severity & Likelihood = Priority**

| Rank | Severity Level | & | Rank | Likelihood | = | Priority | Description |
|---|---|---|---|---|---|---|---|
| 1 | Critical | | 1 | CERTAIN (100%) | | 1 | A fix for the defect is required ASAP.<br><br>(The next Build, must be fixed in current iteration).<br><br>Resolve immediately. |
| 2 | Major | | 2 | HIGH (75%) | | 2 | This defect must be fixed during the current iteration phase.<br><br>Give High Attention. |

| | | | | | |
|---|---|---|---|---|---|
| 3 | Average | 3 | LIKELY (50%) | 3 | This defect must be fixed in the next iteration.<br><br>Normal Queue. |
| 4 | Minor | 4 | LOW (25%) | 4 | This fix is due in a subsequent iteration.<br><br>Low Priority. |
| 5 | Enhancement | 5 | OCCASIONAL (10%) | 5 | An enhancement or suggestion for improvement. |
| 6 | Known Issue | 6 | RARE (1%) | 6 | Monitor for change in status. |

You can also add more combinations as needed giving different combinations of severity and likelihood, e.g., a Critical & Rare = 6 vs. 1 (e.g., 10K bug) …. Several were removed from this example.

## Definitions of QA:
## the good, the bad, and the plain old ugly

If your definition is that QA waits for development to throw code over the wall, and returns a list of the bugs (**the plain old ugly**), please close this book, leave and never return – I can't help you! And yes, I have experience with a Development Manager who believes that; BTY, that company no longer exists. I can quote dozens of formal definitions from as many books and standards ... but in the real world QA is never as simple as the definitions.

• • •

**QA in the real world is never defined as it is in the books. I call it "pushing a string."**

• • •

The definition is important because it allows everyone to think about QA in a similar manner, a common mindset, a common language. By whichever definition you choose, what is most important in the real world is how it is applied and **what QA is actually allowed to do** to meet the primary goal – <u>**help** ensure a quality product/service to the customer</u>. Strickly speaking this is to meet the customer's requirements.

Sometimes "to meet or <u>exceed</u> the customer's expectations" is added. This introduces an <u>untestable</u> component as only if you can document it in a yes/no, true/false (testable) fashion is it a valid requirement.

Please note that in the primary definition, I say to "**help** ensure…" I can't count the number of times I see the definition written without the word **help**. QA alone **cannot** ensure quality! **Quality is the job of veryone!!!** To place the sole burden for quality on QA is to **guarantee failure**!

So the **bad** is a definition that guarantees failure but looks right to many writers?

By now it should be clear that I am referring to QA as the team, group, person/persons, or entity that is **charged with** performing quality assurance as an activity, function or task, not the formal definition of quality assurance itself. IEEE defines the later as:

- A planned and systematic pattern of all actions necessary to provide adequate confidence that an item or product conforms to established technical requirements.
- A set of activities designed to evaluate the **process** by which the products are developed or manufactured. Contrast this with quality control [QC].

Please note that the IEEE definition includes "all actions necessary to…" thereby requiring my addition of the word "help" as quality must then include everyone, not just one entity; It also states "established technical requirements" as I noted above.

Now we have established the basic definition and that we are discussing the entity called quality assurance ... or in the ugly case called testing.

## What QA Is Not!

QA is NOT QC ... you cannot test (inspect) quality into the product!

• • •

**You cannot test (inspect) quality into the product!**

• • •

Attempting to do so at the end of a project is expensive and ineffective.

- For example QC in a Bindery is the process of checking randomly selected printed pieces as they come from the printing press to make sure they meet quality standards and to correct mistakes before continuing – limiting the damage already done. (also see Cost of Quality (CoQ)).

**QC can never do anything to assure the already printed pieces are correct ...** they can provide feedback into QA to help prevent future problems.

## Where is QA Involved?

From the very beginning of the project – a quality product starts with a quality process.

Remember, **GIGO** (garbage in, garbage out).

# How we see each other

Now that we have a definition of quality assurance, whose job is it really – everyone's! Then how come we have so many problems? Well, we all have these things called filters, AKA perceptions. In one picture this idea is captured. Does this look like a group working together with a common goal of quality?

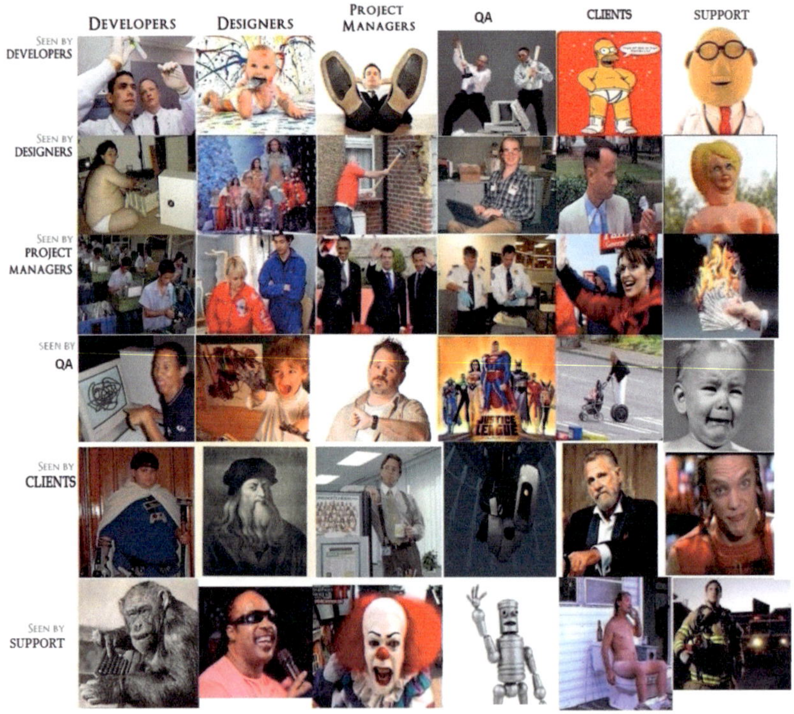


**QA sure has its work cut out I would say ☺**

## Pushing a String

One view of QA is that it is a straight line down a path of actions going from point A to point B as defined by a set of rules, and it is QA who must enforce those rules, no deviations allowed.

• • •

**You can't push a string in a straight line. But you can still help assure a quality product or service.**

• • •

If only the real world was an equation in a math book.

But the real world is not an equation in a math book, and straight lines are rarely if ever found. You can pull a string and keep it straight, but try and do so by pushing it, not going to happen!

I know the definitions, I know how to do QA following the definitions, I know what works and what doesn't ... but I also have never found a company, even those high on the CMMI maturity scale, that follow them precisely. What is a poor QA person to do?

You figure out how to push that string, follow the wiggles and turns (bending of the rules) and do what it takes to help assure a quality product/service TO THE CUSTOMER.

One of the best examples of this I have used is when I had to introduce a formal "development" process, a new set of artifacts and testing procedures. Each developer was required to produce a "requirements/testing" plan and also to fully test their code before installation following that plan. One of my many, many tasks was to oversee that the plans were complete, correct and followed and that testing was performed against the plans; a task I had very limited time for. Installations were daily (Note here, that I am leaving out a whole lot of information about this environment to focus on one single point).

The plans had to be written on PCs in Word format and the development and testing on the production platform, DEC Vax. I had one new developer, who frankly couldn't write good code but was a document wiz, and another one who had never used a PC or word and didn't want to, but whose code was always correct.

In this case, how did I chose to do "quality assurance," i.e., help assure quality, given that I had limited time (I had 28 developers total to deal with and five major job functions, this being only one) while following the process and not breaking the rules? I followed the bends of this string and made the document wiz write grade A perfect documents that could be used for training, development, and testing and I oversaw her progress line by line. As to the coding expert, I accepted a "gentleman's C" level of documentation but demanded perfect code and testing that didn't fail in production without any real oversight – and got it; and he was a happy developer.

While I didn't break any rules, everything was done, I bent them to allow a "workable" standard for each person – creating a Win-Win situation and helped ensure quality for the customer (the actual production application they needed to do their jobs). I took this team from multiple "fire-fighting" installs each day to two planned installs per week with better overall quality.
The moral of this story is that being really good in QA is knowing how and when to bend the rules - without actually breaking them – in the primary goal of a quality product or service to the customer.

## Conclusion

I have laid out a definition of QA, when it should be involved, its overall role in the SDLC, and even admitted to "cheating" to achive the goal of QA, if that is actually cheating , or just being effective, efficient, and productive?

So why then do we have such poor quality? I tell my classes that QA should be the first one(s) hired ... **but they never are**, and usually only much later in the process under a banner of QA/Tester. Just that title tells me what the organization really wants/expects and the related problems I can expect.

**Do you see a problem here?**

Well then at least QA, aka testing, is the last to be laid off, **no** they go second after the training team (the team charged with making sure the reduced staff is cross-trained and can handle the workload in a manner to help ensure quality and productivity!)

## Do we see a problem here?

I said this book can only scratch the surface of what I have seen ... so true!

# Part Four

## ♣The Kitchen Sink♣

• • •

**Life is like a box of chocolates, you never know what you will get.**

**Forest Gump (movie)**

• • •

# Introduction

I wasn't sure where to put these words of wisdom, but they are too good to not include, so I threw them into here. Both are from a movie and movie star named Forrest Gump.

To the first, oh, is it ever so true!

Life is like a box of chocolates,
you never know what you will get.

The second fits what I am talking about in this series to a "T." And has become one of my favorite saying, right after "**and these folks have jobs**!!!" If you understand what I am talking about in this book what else needs to be said.

**Stupid is as Stupid does!**

And before you start calling your lawer to sue me, I use it about myself all the time! What I mean by this phase is when you **decide** to **not** learn from experiences - or worst - not want to!

# The one Dumb Question Is?

**The one dumb question is the one**

**not asked!**

• • •

**The other dumb question is "is my horse hungry" ☺ The only answer is YES!**

• • •

That is what I tell my students all the time and one of the most important concepts I can offer them … and I show lots of pictures of the "dumb" question in everyday life.
If you have a question, then others do too.
Or worst, no one asks questions and quality does not happen and the Cost of Quality (CoQ) goes up.

99% of what I really try to teach my students in class is from real life; they are Master's level students and should know how to read and learn the course materials without much help from me … but I bring the real world experience to the course materials. I tell them what I want them to know when they leave is not how to be the CIS expert, but to know enough to ASK THE RIGHT QUESTIONS to be sure the "expert" they are counting on really is?

My experience tells me that there are a lot of folks out there "asking" the dumb question!

## Are You "Educated?"

I have struggled my whole life to become "educated" in knowing **that** I don't know …. but working to know HOW to find out what I don't know when I need to know it. My struggle continues.
I am the lifelong student …

What bothers me are those who don't/aren't!

**The real definition of education is not what you know but …**

**KNOWING THAT YOU DON'T KNOW.**

I guess this is also part of my belief in CPI (continuous process improvement). Not only to improve the process(es) of what I do, but also the process of how to do it.

I am not sure how "educated" I am – but I'll continue to work on it!!!

## Content vs. Technique

Yes I know I am old fashioned to think of a card catalog to find a book in the library ... but the point is, card catalog, computer lookup system, or even the internet (but that has other issues). If I know what I need to know to find what I want to know, then I do own the contents of the "library" (internet).

• • •

**I can't contain in my head the contents of the library, but teach me to use the card catalog and I own the library**

• • •

This is the topic of the speech I gave in my freshman Speech Communication class. Teach me what I need to know to know how to find out what I don't know and there is nothing I don't know. I become more educated.

## The Law of Unintended Consequences

The law of unintended consequences … another hard lesson for my students and so many folks….

• • •

**For each action there is an opposite and equal reaction.**

***Newton***

• • •

When we make decisions we are usually expecting an obvious consequence that we are looking for. How many of you also look for the possible **unintended consequences**? That is hard(er) to do. You have to ask questions and look at outcomes… what Einstein would call "thought experments."

A class example is when I let my students decide how to allocate the break time (40 minutes over four hours of class). Some always want 10 minutes per hour until I remind them that they can't get across the street and back to get a drink/snack in that time. The unintended consequence of more frequent and shorter breaks.

In the real world, the unintended consequences are not so easy, clear or even singular. Not every decision needs to be analyzed in depth (analysis paralysis) for all its unintended consequences … but it is a way of thinking that should be **practiced and improved**.

## Conclusion

I want to leave this chapter with a few more of the best words of wisdom I can.

- We judge ourselves by our **best intentions**, but we are judged by others by our **last worst acts**.
- The **HARDER** it is – the more **REWARDING** it becomes!
- The only thing that is important is the **RESULT**.
- Often it is a lack of attention to detail that creates the problems … an old fable says: for the want of a nail, the shoe was lost; for the want of the shoe, the horse was lost; for the want of the horse, the general was lost; for the want of the general, the battle was lost; and want of the battle, the war was lost!

So much of this book is about the effects of a lack of attention to details(s)!

And most of all …

**In life EVERYTHING counts!**

**Participation is mandatory!**

• • •

**We have to do it better & we can.**

• • •

# More Words of Wisdom

- Don't make a "dream board" of what you want – make a "nightmare board" of what you **don't** want – that is the real call to ACTION!

- No matter how well you do ... [anything] ... in life – not everyone is going to clap.

- The road to success is always under construction.

- "Experience is a hard teacher because she gives the test first, the lesson afterwards." Vernon Sanders Law (born 1930) ~ Major League Baseball Pitcher

- It can take 12 positive experiences to overcome one negative one. When it comes to customer support/service people tend to tell:
  good = 3 people
  great = 10 people
  bad = 25 people
  an argument happens = 50 people
  a lawsuit = local evening news
  [Rob Swineford – Speak To Win Conference February 20, 2016]

- It is 70-80% cheaper to keep a current customer than to get a new one. The cost to get a new customer is called the **CONVERSION COST**.

- Attitude is the key!

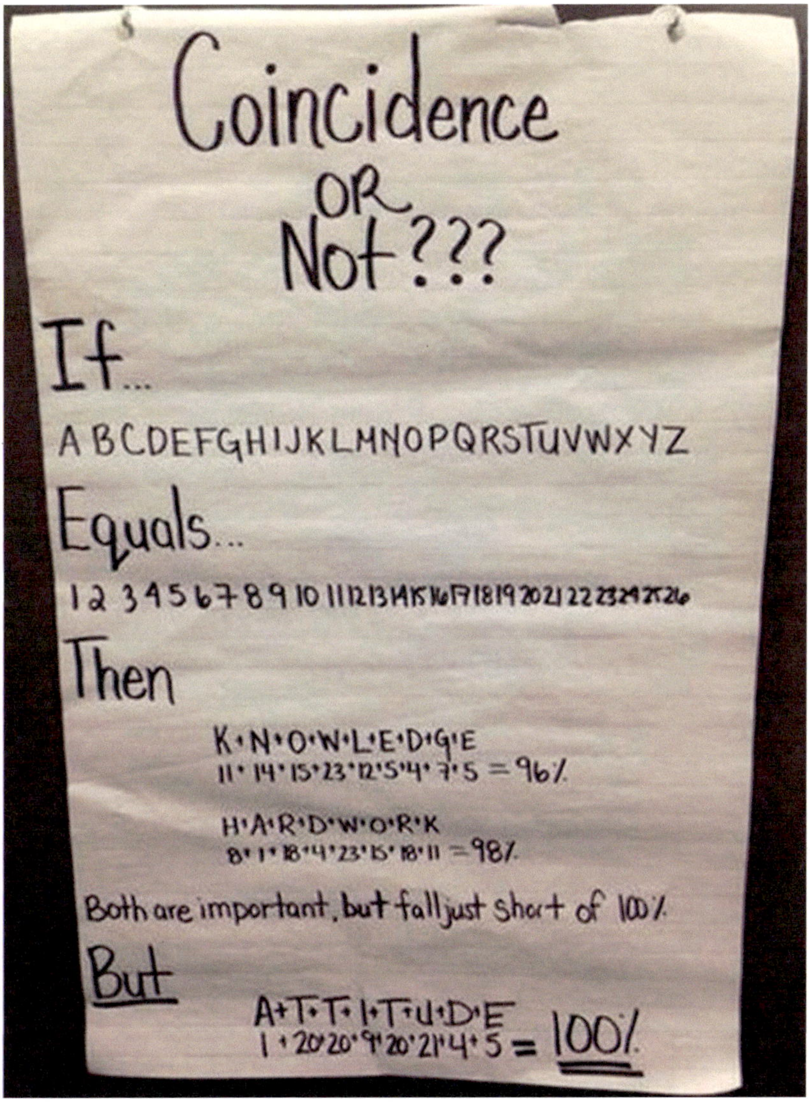
Coincidence
OR
Not???
If...
A B C D E F G H I J K L M N O P Q R S T U V W X Y Z
Equals...
1 2 3 4 5 6 7 8 9 10 11 12 13 14 15 16 17 18 19 20 21 22 23 24 25 26
Then
K•N•O•W•L•E•D•G•E
11•14•15•23•12•5•4•7•5 = 96%
H•A•R•D•W•O•R•K
8•1•18•4•23•15•18•11 = 98%
Both are important, but fall just short of 100%
But
A+T•T•I•T•U•D•E
1+20•20•9•20•21•4•5 = 100%

# ♣Thank You♣

Thank you for taking your valuable time to read my story; the ideas, concepts, techniques, hints, and habits, etc. I discuss work. They have been battle tested!
Remember when it comes to the pursuit of **QUALITY**....

# ♣Feedback♣

If you have any feedback to share about this book, postive or constructive criticism, order of the chapters, or addition chapter(s) you may want added, please contact me (I just may have some experience to share on your topic).

• • •

**If you enjoy the book let me know … I have a lot more stories to tell**

• • •

**I am available to speak on or do on-the-job training for these topics and others.**

**I have hundreds of hours of OJT materials to adapt to your organization and environment that expands on these topics and others.**

# ♣Contact♣

If you want to know more, contact me:

Email: ProfessorWilliam@earthlink.net

Phone: +1 714 785 9297

LinkedIn: www.linkedin.com/in/wrwimberly/

Website: www.williamwimberly.com/books

Made in the USA
Monee, IL
05 November 2026

67378291R00083